Loving and Effective Guidance for Struggling Children
BradMasonCounselor.com

Learn Techniques from a Childhood Counselor
ICYouVideo.com

DIAGNOSIS AUTISM OR ASPERGERS: NOW WHAT?

What to Expect, What to Do, How to Explain!

BRAD MASON, M.ED.

Licensed Professional Counselor,

Licensed Specialist in School Psychology

Print: ISBN: 978-1-947996-00-7
eBook: ISBN: 978-1-947996-01-4
ePub: ISBN: 978-1-947996-02-1
Library of Congress Control Number:
This publication is designed to provide accurate and authoritative information in
regard to the subject matter covered. It is sold with the understanding that the author
or the publisher is not engaged in rendering any type of professional services. If expert
assistance is required, the services of a competent professional should be sought.

1. Autism 2. Aspergers 3. School Psychologists 4. Symptoms 5. Improvement 6. Characteristics 7. Understanding 8. Love
I. Mason, Brad, II. Autism Aspersers: Diagnosis Autism or Aspergers: Now What?
Autism Aspergers: may be purchased at special quantity discounts. Resale opportunities are available for churches, donor programs, fund raising, book clubs, or educational purposes for organizations, churches, schools and universities. For more information
contact Brad: brad@intensivecareforyou.com

Brad Mason, LPC
809 S Elm Street
Georgetown, TX 78626

Intensive Care for You Publishing Speakers Bureau: Have Brad speak at your organi-
zation, workshop, fundraiser or special event.
For information call Brad at (512) 636-6250 or email brad@bradmasoncounselor.com
Cover and interior design by: Megan Van Vuren
Printed in the United States of America
Publishing Consultant: Mel Cohen of Inspired Authors Press LLC http://inspiredau-
thorspress.com/
Publisher: Intensive Care for You Publishing, LLC
Autism Aspergers Website: http://intensivecareforyou.com/

DEDICATION

This book is dedicated to all those who have suffered needlessly due to misunderstanding, ignorance, and fear.

FOREWORD

I read some years ago in my NASP (National Association of School Psychologists) handbook that "autism is a lifelong disease." I think this is misleading from two standpoints. First, it's not a disease. It doesn't get worse as time goes on, it doesn't mean the person is sick, and you can't die from it. Second, while there may or may not be a "cure," the symptoms of autism can and usually do improve over time and with therapy and effort. Rather than viewing autism as a disease, I would encourage you to think of it as a difference that may at times cause some "dis-ease," and at other times may produce miracles of innovation and creativity.

I made this book for you. I wrote this to spread understanding, acceptance, and appropriate assistance for all the people who have symptoms of autism or Aspergers syndrome. I have observed and interviewed some special people who have overcome a great many challenges, with help and special parenting, to find themselves comfortable with who they are and reconciled with the criticisms and judgments they received from others. I want you to become that person for someone else, that person who shows them compassion, always thinks well of them, and continues to encourage and support them even when unexpected behaviors are occurring. Hopefully, you've known at least one person in your life who always saw you as good and capable and took the time to lift you up so that you could become your better possible self.

> It's not a disease. It doesn't get worse as time goes on, it doesn't mean the person is sick.

v

I think God made people different for a reason. Look at Einstein, Edison, da Vinci, and Mozart.

Who do you think came up with and created rockets and computers, anyway?

Either you or someone you know has autism. I hope this will help you expand your limits and overcome obstacles. You have no idea how much you have to offer and how far you and those you love can go until you stop limiting yourself. With understanding, love, and therapeutic social connections we can all transform and leap into a happy, healthy, and purposeful life. I've seen this happen over and over again in my practice.

> Who do you think came up with and created rockets and computers, anyway?

This is not intended to be the be-all and end-all manual for autism and Aspergers syndrome. It is meant to give an overview that explains why people with this condition have the difficulties and unexpected behaviors they display. We'll explore resources and techniques for getting started on making it better for those who have autism or Aspergers syndrome, as well as their families. You should come away with an overview of the characteristics of autism spectrum disorder and have some practical strategies and good resources to help you remediate or compensate for these difficulties and help those on the spectrum do what is expected more often and enjoy a higher quality of life. You can also find a video course that goes with this book as well as additional resources at www.intensivecareforyouvideo.com.

TABLE OF CONTENTS

— Chapter 1 —

DIAGNOSIS

Do I want it or not?

What if my child sort of fits the
diagnostic criteria but not exactly?

DIFFERENT KINDS OF AUTISM

First, we have straight-up autism. Then, for those who meet most but not all criteria for autism, we have pervasive developmental disorder, not otherwise specified, or PDD-NOS. Aspergers syndrome used to be in the diagnostic manual as falling under the umbrella of autism spectrum disorder in the United States, but now it doesn't. When they removed Aspergers syndrome, they added social communication disorder, or SCD. You also may come across the term "high-functioning autism," which is not really an official diagnostic category, but more of a way of describing a person as having autism and also being fairly verbal and able to participate in an academic school curriculum. Autismspeaks.org has a good listing of the official

DSM-V criteria if you want to see it. Since this book is meant to help you understand and manage the real-life symptoms of a person with autism, Aspergers, or one who possesses characteristics of either, and not as a manual for making diagnoses, I don't want you to spend your time reading too much about diagnosing. That's best left to professionals in the school or healthcare industry.

Don't get too caught up in it. All of these diagnostic categories are made up by groups of people. They are not perfect; many people fit into multiple categories. Few people fit into any one diagnostic category perfectly. If you like to do research and you review criteria for autism, Aspergers, OCD, PDD-NOS, SCD, CAPD, anxiety, bipolar disorder, ADHD, ADD, and sensory integration disorder, trying to figure out which one or ones a person really "has" can get confusing in a hurry.

To me, it makes more sense for families and professionals to develop a vocabulary that conveys a person's strengths and weaknesses in operational and understandable terms. For example, if someone has trouble adapting to changes in routine, then let's just say that, and then help them work on ways in which they can be more flexible. We can also help them to prepare for changes or avoid them to make things easier.

WHAT IS A DIAGNOSIS GOOD FOR? DO I WANT IT?

I'm just going to share a few brief observations that might help you if you have questions or concerns about a diagnosis and what a diagnosis is good for.

A diagnosis is good for receiving reimbursement for services through insurance, as well as becoming classified for special education services in a public school. A diagnosis is also good for communicating with other people about what to expect, broadly speaking, when meeting and working with the individual diagnosed. A diagnosis can also point to a body of literature and resources that have been helpful to use with other people who have had similar characteristics. Sort of a shortcut for what to do and what to expect.

Can you use this book with someone who hasn't been diagnosed with autism but still appears to have some of the features? Yes you can! If you suspect a child may have autism or Aspergers, I would encourage you to seek testing, either with their school or with an outside professional, which will usually be a psychologist who gives a battery of tests and spends a couple of days testing, interviewing, and writing up a report. Scores on a single rating scale alone should never be used to definitively say that a person does or does not fall on the autism spectrum.

Another issue to consider relevant to diagnosis is when or if you should tell the child receiving the diagnosis and when or if you should tell their classmates. Since every child and situation is different, it wouldn't work to specify an age at which you tell them. I think you should consider their level of cognitive and social development. Also, consult with other people, such as parents of children on the spectrum, teachers, maybe a counselor, school psychologist, speech therapist, and so on. See what they say and decide what you think is best.

Just remember that if you don't address an established diagnosis with the person who received it, problems may occur. The person may deny any problems with their performance and conduct, thus refusing to take responsibility and work to improve themself. They may also conclude something very unflattering about themselves, like they are lazy, or stupid, or worthless, or crazy.

The same thing goes for classmates. If they don't have an explanation for unexpected behaviors and mannerisms, they may make similar insulting errors about the child you care about, and then they may avoid, ridicule, or bully them.

ARE THEY GIFTED OR DO THEY HAVE ASPERGERS?

Gifted children can tend to be intense, emotionally and in their patterns of interest. They can have trouble socializing with age-peers, worry about things usually only adults worry about, and have difficulty organizing and staying focused. Gifted children may have difficulty with everyday problem-solving and poor motor coordination. In other words, characteristics of children who are gifted and children who have high-functioning autism or Aspergers syndrome overlap.

So which one is it? It depends on how much their challenges disrupt their environment and their ability to function in groups, in school, and at home. It also depends on the level of support they need. A diagnosis can help get more support services and reimbursement by insurance companies.

WHAT IS TWICE EXCEPTIONAL?

To make things a little more complicated, a person can also be twice exceptional, or 2e, meaning they are both gifted and have autism, or OCD, or ADHD, or dyslexia, or anxiety, as well as any other mental and emotional conditions. Sometimes one condition masks the other. For example, a child may be autistic and gifted, to the degree that their autism symptoms mask their giftedness, and they are so bright that their giftedness hides their autism symptoms. They may be bright enough that they can compensate well for their autism, or their dyslexia, and appear fairly normal on the outside to most people, while few people realize the struggle they undergo internally to overcome their challenges and perform as expected. Personally, I'd rather describe myself or my child as gifted versus autistic, so if intensive supports are not needed and they can do well enough with just, say, good professional counseling support, the question to this dilemma may be: which do you prefer?

14

What if a family member doesn't believe in the diagnosis? What if my father, mother, or spouse doesn't believe the diagnosis?

Typically, moms are more proactive. They may say, "Let's do something now; I think something might be wrong." Dads are more likely to minimize and resist, by stating, "Oh, there's nothing wrong with him. He's just being a boy. I acted the same way when I was that age." Grandparents are sometimes of the opinion that if they were just disciplined appropriately and more firmly, they wouldn't act that way. They may feel that nothing is actually wrong with the child; they are just exhibiting bad behavior. Well, have them read this book. Suggest to them the possibility of spending a day with the youngster at day care, to see how it goes, how much help they need, and if they are fitting in with age-peers or not. Family members who share the same characteristics may have a unique sense of what normal is, and see a person on the spectrum as being normal for their family!

MORE TIPS FOR WORKING WITH NON-BELIEVERS

Remove the label and keep working on the skills and behavior anyway. "Every kid has their quirks, and these are his." "She responds better if you ask her this way."

Remember that in the grandparents' day, autism meant low functioning and little language.

Remember that people often fear what they don't understand.

Agree to disagree.

GRIEF AND DENIAL ABOUT A DIAGNOSIS

Everyone grieves in a different way and on their own timetable. Normally, people pass through stages of anger, denial, and bargaining. Ideally, they reach the point of acceptance, but this can be difficult for some, and in some cases may never completely happen. Imagine facing the worry, or even the reality, of your child not being able to hold a job, live independently, get married, have friends, and/or graduate from college—many of the successes parents earnestly hope to see their offspring achieve. Who wants to think about such things?

CASE STUDY

I know a man in his thirties who has autism and possesses the mental age of about six, I believe. His parents are still waiting and wondering when he will "get his act together, grow up, and get a job." This man—let's say his name is Peter—received special education as a student with autism and an intellectual disability in a self-contained setting. Perhaps because Peter's autism enables him to be fairly good with computers, his parents still think he is high functioning. They still hope one day things will "click," and Peter will start solving problems effectively and stop having rages and tantrums that require 24/7 staffing and prevent him from visiting his parents in their home.

An example of his problem-solving difficulty would be that when he was still in high school, he wanted to join the military. He wrote probably hundreds of letters demanding that his autism be "taken off" his record so that he would be eligible for military service.

Peter does not drive, does not have a job, and needs prompts to take his medications and keep up with hygiene routines. His parents have wavered between bargaining and denial about the extent of Peter's limitations. Their hopes and beliefs that he is high functioning is a form of denial. Thinking he will one day get his act together or receive the right behavior plan or medicine so that he can become more normal and intelligent represents a bargaining phase.

Bargaining can take the form of "When we find the right therapy, this will go away," or "Someday he will finally wake up and get his act together." Whatever makes the limitations that have not been accepted no longer so. I think we are best off if we maintain hope and work to sustain faith that things will be okay. I also know from my years of practice that everyone can and does get better eventually. So please don't get me wrong. I'm not at all saying just give up. I'm saying never give up, but be reasonable and try to accept your loved ones as they are where they are now.

— Chapter 2 —

MIND-BLINDNESS: THEORY OF MIND

Theory of mind, or TOM, means understanding that people have different agendas, experiences, plans, feelings, and ideas. Someone with disruptions in the development of TOM may tend to view the world as if we are all participating in the same stream of consciousness—theirs. This explains why a person on the spectrum may start a conversation somewhere in the middle without providing an introduction or context. Why they might be upset if your plan or opinion differs from theirs. Why they might, at times, treat others as if they should perform their will as if the separate person were an extension of the spectrum person's body, like one of their hands. Wouldn't you be frustrated if one of your arms or legs suddenly quit working and wouldn't follow your instructions?

On the milder end, we may have insistence that an opinion is a fact, neglecting to ask for help (because they don't think about the fact that others may know things they don't), and trouble with perspective taking. On the severe end of disrupted development of TOM we could have a person who doesn't recognize others as beings to interact with at all.

Characteristics of poorly developed theory of mind could include difficulty with the following examples:

- *Literal*: **Concrete and fail to interpret figures of speech/idioms. Tend to split hairs, such as arguing that it is *not* 4:00 because it's only 3:58.**

- *Empathy*: **May not notice how others are feeling or may not modify their behavior to keep others feeling good.**

- *Perspective taking*: **May stay stuck in their perspective and insist others are wrong if they don't agree; may even try to make others agree they are right.**

- *Persuading*: **May demand and insist rather than using tact and diplomacy to influence others.**

- *Compromise*: **Exactly my way or the highway.**

- *Honest to a fault*: **How much food did you have to eat to get that fat?**

- *Conflict resolution*: **Lacking diplomacy and tact needed for resolving interpersonal problems.**

- *Get overwhelmed:* **Being around others because they are working so hard to figure them out, rather than using intuition.**

You may also notice the following characteristics:

- **not knowing when to be embarrassed.**

- **having trouble figuring out how others will feel or react to them.**

- **may appear rude and disrespectful to others.**

- **may be paranoid because others seem so unpredictable.**

- **trouble understanding deception; being easily deceived or taken advantage of.**

- **starting in the middle of a conversation—think you know what they know.**

- **don't realize or read the cues that others aren't interested in monologues.**

What are some ways to help a person develop better perspective-taking skills, more empathy, and greater consideration of how they impact and shape the experience and feelings of the people with whom they share space?

To help with being overly literal and splitting hairs, I like to teach the kids what splitting hairs means. I have them think about trying to split a hair, and show them on a clock with hands and numbers the difference between 3:58 and 4:00. Are those two times pretty much the same or not?

Parents are encouraged to use keywords like "splitting hairs," which become anchoring experiences when their kid is "making a mountain out of a molehill" again. It can be entertaining to conjure and draw images to go with idioms for fun—a "brook chuckling over its stony bed," "hurting like fire," and "can we get on the same page here?"

After laughing, we can think about what this phrase REALLY does mean. Apples to Apples is a game that makes you look at how non-identical terms could be somewhat the same, even though not exactly so.

More importantly, you can ask kids to make inferences based on non-verbal clues as to what a person's plan might be. For instance, if two people are standing close to one another while talking, and a third person approaches and watches them but doesn't speak, what is the silent person's intention?

To help with being overly literal and splitting hairs, I like to teach the kids what splitting hairs means

That's right, they want to say or ask something; they are using their body position to give the speaking people awareness that they want something from them, without verbally interrupting. You can watch for these teachable moments while at home or in the community. You can use cartoons as well, pausing on a character before they speak or do something, and then asking the child to use the clues to guess what the character is thinking or feeling.

Getting someone with a literal-thinking style to make guesses can be tough because many of these folks do not like gray areas—and you can't REALLY know what someone is thinking or planning, but you are expected to make a guess or ask if you are not sure. Socializing is really based on a lot of guesswork, much of which you can't be completely sure of. Most of us do it automatically without thinking about it, but without this guesswork and scaffolding of assumptions, we really can't socialize effectively at all. You have to be willing and able to watch people and make educated guesses about their thoughts, feelings, and intentions.

You are a Social Detective by Michelle Garcia-Winner and Pamela Crooke is a good book to teach younger children—from the developmental ages of about four to eight years—how to use what they see and hear to do what is expected and how doing what is unexpected can impact how others feel about them in a negative way.

I also teach kids to defer, which means to allow other people to think they are right even when you think they are wrong—just let it go and don't continue to insist or argue. Sometimes it's better to allow someone to think they are right even though you don't agree, so the play or conversation can move forward.

Socializing is really based on a lot of guesswork

Getting someone who is not in the habit of thinking about how others are thinking about them and modifying their behavior to keep others having good thoughts about them will often take many, many repeated trials. Using behavior modification techniques to increase motivation will help too. (For examples of how this would look, please see my video course, "Behavior Management at its Best," or sign up for the free mini-course on behavior management in the *Resources for Free* section at intensivecareforyou.com. You can take away some valuable concepts and techniques that can help you every day.)

For a greater grasp of deception I like to give kids in my groups some real money and teach them to play poker. I explain bluffing, ways to recognize a bluff, and how to manage your nonverbal communication to make a bluff. I explain that people out there in the world will try to deceive you to get your money. There are also some games you can play with them, such as <u>Fib or Not</u> and <u>Fact or Crap</u>. In <u>Fib or Not</u>, the kids have to either tell a story that is true but try to convince their playmates the story is a lie, or they have to tell a story that is a lie but convince their playmates it is true.

Another concept related to being literal or black and white with interpretations of honesty is the "social fake." Many of the children and young adults I have worked with are extremely uncomfortable with not being genuine and honest. You may be thinking right now, what's wrong with being genuine and honest? Consider these social scenarios. Your best friend enters the room. You notice she has a new haircut, and you think it looks terrible on her. How do you know if it's okay to be honest? Would it ever be a better choice to lie or try to say something nice about her appearance? How do you judge with whom and when you tell the truth and when you change the truth a little bit? You consider what you know about the person based on past experience and try to predict their reaction. Then you weigh your options carefully. Here's another example of the social fake. You're at a party and you are introduced to someone new. You are not sure if you really want to meet them or if you will like them. If you convey your uncertainty and doubt with your body language, you may cross your arms, hold yourself at a greater distance from them, and look away from them more than expected. How will they interpret your behavior? (This person doesn't like me or want to talk to me.) So it's better to let on with your posture, tone, and words, by making eye contact, smiling, and acting as if you are happy and interested. This is expected! Doing something unexpected will likely cause them to have weird or uncomfortable thoughts about you. Act happy and interested, and you may "fake it until you make it." You will either

> How will they interpret your behavior?

find some common ground and interest with the new person and if not, you should create a reason to excuse yourself, and say something possibly not quite true. "Oh, look, there's Pete, I really need to go talk to him. It was really great meeting you, and I hope to see you again!"

A related concept is *central coherence*. Central coherence refers to what is typically a natural process for the mind to take in details and create a meaningful concept that explains how the details fit together to form an idea. What happens if a mind memorizes or just perceives details without trying to make sense of them and link pieces together to draw conclusions? You get into trouble with big-picture thinking, reading comprehension, and understanding and predicting the behavior and intentions of others.

Soooo... how else can you help someone develop this ability?

Ask questions while reading to a child, "What is this about?" or "What do you think will happen next?" or "How do you think the characters are thinking/feeling?" "How will they react and what sort of plan might they come up with?" "What is the problem and how could it be solved?" You can do the same thing while watching cartoons and movies. You can even pause and see if the child can guess the feelings as well. You can provide prompts to "get outside their head" to use their eyes, ears, and brain to gather information from the environment. You can ask them to figure out what others are doing, what they expect from others in the same group or space, or how they can help.

Ask questions while reading to a child

There's a book called *Teaching Children with Autism to Mind Read* by Julie A. Hadwin, Patricia Howlin, and Simon Baron-Cohen. It presents pictures of people in particular situations—for instance, a snake in front of a girl—and asks how she will feel. This facilitates predicting others' emotions based on a situation. The next step has pictures and stories where a character's desires are indicated and then they either do or do not get what they want. This helps to de-

"What is this about?" or "What do you think will happen next?"

velop the understanding that people are happy when they get what they want and not happy when they don't. Then they throw in a curve. What if Billy wants a plane for his birthday, but he thinks he is getting a kite; how will he feel then? How will he feel when he finds out he is getting a plane after all? So we learn to predict others' emotions based on what their beliefs are.

Another way to develop perspective taking and big-picture thinking is to ask them to guess someone's plan based on an observed action. For example, if someone has trash in their hand and they are headed for the trash can, what do you think their plan is? What is their intention? One child is swinging and laughing while another is standing close by, crying with clenched fists. Why is one crying, and what could they want?

Social skills groups can help here too. It makes sense to me to say that some kids may not develop empathy until they have experienced feeling successful having fun with others in a group. If it's more rewarding playing by yourself, why should you care what others think and feel? But when someone discovers how much MORE fun and exciting it can be in a shared experience, they start to develop some buy-in to working at being with others and caring about their thoughts and feelings.

Some of my favorite and most effective social skills and perspective-taking resources come from Michelle Garcia-Winner (www.socialthinking.com) such as the Superflex curriculum; you can see me using some of it in my social skills video course. I attempt to teach social and perspective-taking concepts as many ways as I can to try and get the point across—utilizing role-play, comic strips, video modeling, charts, and stories—coaching in the context of real interactions with other kids. About fifteen years ago I was facilitating a group with kids from the ages of six to seven. This one really bright dragon-loving girl kept bringing really cool stuff in her backpack to play with before the start of the group session. The other kids wanted to check out the items as well; however, this little girl would not share. Finally, we started to play with some great things of our own. When she asked if she could participate, we said no and kept exclaiming how fun it was to play with our items. She got mad and asked us why. We explained this was what it was like for the others when she brought out her cool stuff and wouldn't share. The next time we met, she presented an interesting light-up toy. When the other kids asked if they could see it more closely, she said "NO" again. We reminded her about her experience in the previous meeting. She groaned but then finally shared. She needed to experience for herself what it was like to get treated badly by someone else, and she needed to modify her behavior accordingly.

— Chapter 3 —

HIGH ANXIETY AND STRESS

If you had trouble understanding what others expect of you, thought about things differently than those around you, got overwhelmed by your sensory experience of just being in the world, and received repeated messages that you either were doing something wrong or weren't doing what you were supposed to do, you'd get nervous and or mad, too, wouldn't you?

Remember, we are probably talking about someone who has a history of failure and rejection and tends to be a perfectionist and an extremist (it's all good or all bad). This person uses their intellect rather than intuition to figure out social situations, so they are working harder and getting overwhelmed more easily. I have a whole video course for you at intensivecareforyou.com about anxiety, as well as self-esteem.

I would imagine the concept of feelings could be troublesome for some people on the spectrum. Not that I don't think they feel—

quite the contrary, in fact. I believe that often they may feel much more intensely, and consequently need to escape others or block themselves from feeling so as to prevent themselves from becoming overwhelmed. The part that is difficult about feeling is how do we know what *anxious* feels like? It's not the same for me as it is for you. Emotional arousal is the same across many feelings within the same person as it is different between persons. I think we first detect our arousal level and then use the context to give the feeling a name. I'm watching someone I don't like driving a car I wish I had, and my body is telling me I'm stressed or worried or mad or something. Hmmm, I must be jealous. See what I mean?

Tony Attwood wrote some very good workbooks called *Exploring Feelings*. One of my favorite parts is that he has a menu to choose from for what your body does when you are having an emotional response. Do you develop sweaty palms, itchy skin, or tight muscles? Tony also presents cognitive-behavioral strategies for dealing with feelings, such as his list of poisonous thoughts and antidotes to poisonous thoughts. For example, "I never do anything right," is a poisonous thought, whereas "Sometimes I make mistakes, but most of the time I get it right, and I can try again or get help" would be an antidote to that poisonous thought. Lastly, I like his "emotional toolbox" idea, with categories of tools you can use to help manage or dissolve anxious feelings:

- *Social Tools:* You can talk to someone you trust.

- *Thinking Tools*: Grade the size of the problem on a scale from 1–10. Then use your self-talk and think to yourself, "That's okay, I can handle it."

- *Activity Tools:* Do something you love; go outside and run until you feel better.

- *Relaxation tools:* Guided imagery, breathing, hot bath, meditation.

- *Other tools:* **Special interests, medicine, humor.**

- *Inappropriate tools:* **These are things you may do when worried or stressed, but they don't solve the problem or they make things worse.**

The Incredible 5-Point Scale by Buron and Curtis, 2012, is great also. It helps teach gradations—rather than all or nothing scenarios, like being happy or having a meltdown with no in-between phases. It shows how to develop an emotional vocabulary. If you want to see how I use it, please see my video course, "Anxiety and Children" or "Anger and Children." By the way, often I find that underneath what looks like anger is actually anxiety. Anger is the behavior we see that the person is using to make things work the way they want, because they are anxious about deviations from what they want or expect.

I like teaching thinking strategies the best because they are powerful and portable (you can bring them with you as long as you can remember them). They are also private (nobody can see you using them). Your thoughts are so powerful that they create your reality. It's not what happens that creates your feelings, it's how you think about what happens. It could start raining right now, and I could get really mad about it and think, "No, it can't be raining. This is going to ruin everything; how will I go fishing now?" I could stay mad about it all day. Or, I could get happy about it instead. I could think, "Hey, this is great. My grass and garden will grow better, and maybe the river will fill up so I can go kayaking!" And so I could be happy about the rain all day. Here we have the same event in both cases: the rain. Do you see how different thoughts equal different feelings?

For younger children, the book *Thotso* by Avery, R. (2008) can help you teach how this works. It introduces the idea that your brain can make thoughts that make you smile and thoughts that make you hurt—smiling thoughts and boo-boo thoughts. When you have a boo-boo thought, you can make a smiling thought to help yourself feel better. For older kids, there is a game called <u>Land of Psymon</u> which has cards, sort of like Pokémon cards, representing categories of unwanted or incorrect thoughts. For example, the Extremist tries to make you think that if a situation is not perfect, then it is terrible. Then there is the Wish-fish, who teaches you smarter ways of thinking and reminds you that things are never all good or all bad; we can wish they were perfect and be content with what we get or do.

For adults or teens, we can use cognitive distortions. You will find these categories of thinking errors located in the *Resources for Free* page at intensivecareforyou.com. You can also sign up for the free mini-course with video and have some forms and templates emailed to you.

You will also find in the *Resources for Free* page a menu of "Stress Triggers," "Stress Signs," and "Stress Management Strategies." Have the child you are caring for highlight the items from the menu that resonate with them. Use this to identify triggers and possibly eliminate them from the environment. This practice also helps them develop greater awareness of when they are getting stressed, before it's too late and they start acting out. They will have a menu of strategies for managing their emotional responses and caring for themselves in appropriate ways.

> Your brain can make thoughts that make you smile and thoughts that make you hurt

There are also lifestyle adjustments you can make, such as preventative measures to keep stress at bay. These might include: exercising, taking a daily nap, meditating or praying, eating healthy, avoiding or reducing stress triggers, spending time having fun, scheduling downtime, hanging out with friends, and maintaining regular sleeping habits.

— Chapter 4 —

BULLYING

By middle school, if not earlier, humans in our culture, for whatever reason, begin to fear and sometimes target and criticize anyone who is different, even if the differences are small. These variances could include: skin tone, the sound of a voice, the structure of facial features, or how hair is cut and groomed. These nuances of appearance and behavior, and the rejection of an individual who looks or sounds different, make up what we call culture, and establish how we identify someone as a member of our group, or tribe, and one who is not a member, or an outcast. Being an outcast and not having a group to identify with for protection is threatening. For one, outcast or non-member status invites the possibility of attack from groups or tribes that strike out at non-members as a way to defend territory and resources.

Human beings are fragile. We are born vulnerable, unable to survive alone. We are dependent on the goodwill and care of others for our survival. Even as adults, most of us would have difficulty surviving in the wilderness alone. We live in groups with rules; we call this civilization for a reason. We specialize. We find a way to contribute to others, and we offer our services that are needed or wanted and provide to other group members in exchange for goods and services we may want or need for ourselves. Most of us don't know how to make the shoes we wear, construct the roof over our head, or grow the food for our table. Many of us don't know how to birth babies. Most of us don't know how to develop medicines or provide defense against attackers. We each do our thing so we can get someone else to do the things we don't have the skills or training for. This is how we live. Nearly everything we get or enjoy is derived from relationship; our status with others is important and helps give value to what we can do for others in exchange for what we need.

Unfortunately, I have seen children who were bullied mercilessly at school by the same kids year after year. Add to that the way some kids on the spectrum can hold a grudge, focusing on one negative and ignoring all other positives in their life. In addition, they can have a friend who does them wrong one time and then suddenly becomes the enemy, and there is no flexibility for forgiveness.

Bullying is a natural way to establish dominance and gain favor with peers. When the dominant member of a group, or a member trying to curry favor with the rest of the group and elevate their own status, can put down, ridicule, or ostracize someone else, they are actually arguing their position in the social hierarchy. So some bullying is a fairly common behavior exhibited by popular kids. What to do? For one thing, you can normalize it; a little teasing is normal and not something to freak out about. Sometimes it's just good-natured ribbing. This is, after all, the way a lot of grownup men talk to each other all the time. There is a website where you can purchase useful materials, as well as obtain some for free, to help with bullying. Bullies2buddies.com focuses on treatment for the victim rather than the perpetrator.

My sister-in-law, Jen Mason, who teaches self-defense at a university in Minneapolis, says they prefer the word "target" instead of "victim" because the implied powerlessness is removed. They also use the word "offender" instead of "perpetrator."

There once was a man who liked to go to the park and toss breadcrumbs. The longer he walked through the park, and the more breadcrumbs he threw out, the more pigeons flocked around him. The man did not like this, and he was very upset by the pigeons flying all around him. The man was afraid, angry, and felt very wronged by the pigeons' behavior, fluttering all about him, making their sounds. "Why," he asked, "won't they just leave me alone?" "Don't they know I don't like them all around me like this?"

Because the man did not like these pigeons and felt they were wrong to fly and strut all around him, he began going to the park even more often and throwing out more breadcrumbs in his defiance and outrage. This, of course, encouraged the pigeons, and made more of them approach him more often.

What advice would you give the man who liked to go to the park and throw out breadcrumbs? What behaviors do you think are like breadcrumbs to bullies, encouraging them to come around more often and do more of what you do not like? What could you do instead?

Consider treating the victims rather than the bullies. To me, there is something very strange about punishing bullies, and we know from research that this does not work. Why would it? Isn't it modeling using your power against someone less powerful to make them behave the way you want? And so the bully, once punished, after doing his time in ISS or whatever, goes out and takes from others with lessor power he or she doesn't approve of.

Please don't misunderstand. I'm not saying we should blame the targets of bullying for the bad behavior. I am saying that if you look at research about bullying prevention, the programs that target the bullies don't work. I am saying we should empower children who have suffered with skills to stand up and solve the problem without violence or making things worse.

EARLY WARNING SIGNS
i.e. The Precursors of Bullying Behavior

- Irritability, impatience, moodiness from an early age.
- Tendency to perceive others as having hostile intent—meanly making them lose with hostile intent, rather than just trying to win as expected in the game.
- Quick retaliation for real or imagined threats.
- Trouble identifying feelings. Instead of effectively communiating, acts out
- Difficulty recognizing their pain and the pain of others.
- Abusive or neglectful home environment.

DEVELOPING CLASS RULES TO
DEAL WITH BULLYING

- Discuss what bullying is and get examples from the students.
- Teach that if everyone sticks together, no one is left out and a bully can't isolate or pick on anyone.
- Teach the difference between tattling and telling. Telling is when something could be dangerous and someone could get hurt. Otherwise, write it or draw it and put it in the tattle box. Letting the teacher know that someone is being verbally or physically abusive is not tattling.
- Present and discuss these rules about bullying:
  - » *We agree no student will be permitted to bully another student.*
  - » *We agree we will help any student being bullied by telling them to stop and/or get help from an adult.*

> » *We agree not to exclude any student from an activity in school or on the playground.*
- **Post the rules in the classroom.**

The creator of bullies2buddies, Izzy Kalman, says that programs that focus on the perp don't work. Think about it. The school punishes the bully, and guess what? The idea that you cause discomfort for someone less powerful than you is reinforced. They get out of in-school suspension and go right out and do it again. Izzy teaches six rules to follow, including refusing to let the other person make you upset and treating the words of everyone as if they are words from your best friend. Don't fight back; if you are hurt, then say so. He teaches that bullying is all about winning and losing. If you stay calm and in control, you look like the winner, and the bully ends up looking like a jerk. A couple of sentences don't do his program justice. It's a good program and is part of what I use in my clinic. Most of the kids on the spectrum who come to my clinic have had trouble with bullying. Many are to the point where they are refusing to go back to their school. Often their reactions to bullying are getting them into trouble.

You can help by teaching them to discriminate between less harmful teasing and when they are truly being hurt or exploited—laughed at or laughed with? Is this coming from someone who usually treats you well? You can check it out with them by asking, "Are you seriously trying to put me down and hurt me, or are you just joking around?"

Telling a teacher is not always the best answer. It can backfire when the accused bully gets in trouble and takes revenge and when other students disrespect the tattletale. If you fight back, even if you get in trouble or get beat up, at least you may stop the problem and earn respect—from others and for yourself. Sometimes fighting back, while not the school's solution, tends to be a better solution socially. If it were my kid, and they had been bullied by the same person, tattled to school staff, and the bullying kept happening, I'd tell school officials. I have five boys, and one of them is on the spectrum. I've said to them all, "The next time they try to hurt you, either punch them hard right in the nose or kick them in the private parts. You will get in trouble at school but not at home." My kids liked being given this option, but none of them have used it yet. I think they just preferred to not show a big reaction or make a big deal out of it, and then the bully moved on to more reactive targets.

> I think they just preferred to not show a big reaction or make a big deal out of it, and then the bully moved on to more reactive targets

It can be really hard to ascertain remotely whether your kid is really being put down or they are being included in the normal jocular banter that occupies the hallways of public schools. It's good to have something to say back if you are in front of peers and you want to preserve your pride.

HOW DO YOU TEACH A TARGET TO DEAL WITH BULLYING?

First of all, don't tell them they are the victim; use the word target instead. There is an important semantic difference here.

Don't make yourself a big target.

Does your posture show weakness and invite a bully? Practice proper posture, have confidence in your tone of voice, pitch your voice lower, and pay attention to your gait and style of walking. A boy shouldn't be prancing around with his hands held higher than his waist. He should have his chest out, shoulders back, chin high, and gaze direct. He should not confrontationally glare, nor be looking away fearfully.

Observe the student and interview peers for any other behaviors they may be engaging in that may make them a big target for bullying. Point out that sometimes we fake it until we make it. Play poker with some loose change so they understand how to bluff.

Don't show a big reaction.
Remember the pigeons and breadcrumbs story.

Build self-esteem.
For more information and techniques for self-esteem, see my video course.

Remind them that nobody can make them feel anything without their permission and cooperation.
Tell the student you want to play a game with them. Explain that you want them to imagine that you have put $500 or even $1,000 on the corner of the table or desk. Say that they can win the money by not getting upset while you make fun of them and call them names. Ask them if they could win. If they don't smile right away, say, "Sure, you could; you'd sit there smiling thinking about all the money you are getting from this fool who is making it easy for you. See? As long as you decide that there is no way I am going to make you feel upset, I can't make you." I've done this scores of times and nearly all the kids get it, unless they are really concrete or entrenched and trained in victim mentality. Refuse to give them the power to make you mad.

Do not defend yourself from verbal taunts, accusations, or name calling.
It takes two to create a conflict, and if

> Remind them that nobody can make them feel anything without their permission and cooperation

37

you defend yourself, an enemy is automatically created.

Hit them back? Well, that's a controversial answer, and so you'd better not say that if you work for the school, especially if you haven't consulted with the parents yet. Personally, I trained my kids to hit back if they are being hurt and can't get away. Punch them in the nose or kick them in the balls, if they have them. Telling is the teacher answer, but socially this can backfire through disrespect into more bullying, and many students have reported to me that they told the teacher and it didn't help. At least if you fight back, even if you get beat up, the bully and your peers will respect you after and the bullying may stop. So socially, and for the target's own self-respect, trying to get at least one really good lick in on the bully may be the better answer if the target is getting physically hurt and abused. I definitely think you should alert the parents to the problem, and inquire how they plan to advise their child.

Get a big friend.
Help the student to get a group to hang out with to reduce isolation and create more safety. Maybe introduce them to a group you think they could fit in with; ask the group to take the person in. Maybe it's a group of kids who are sometimes labeled as misfits, emos, nerds, jocks, hicks, rockers, or whatever.

Teach about victim mentality.
Give up your idea of rights and fairness. Are there laws that make people treat each other well and make the world fair? Are their laws against teasing? Are there laws that say you have the right to a life of fairness? How about in nature? If you are a little fuzzy creature running around in the woods, do you have the right not to be eaten by a bigger fuzzy creature? No, it's just that whatever happens—happens. You have to make your own way, and if you expect life to be fair, you

are setting yourself up for a lifetime of disappointment. Learn to say to yourself, "I wish life was fair all the time, and I'm glad that usually it is and most of the time I am treated nicely. I can handle a few problems now and then." Point out that to believe "I must be treated fairly and I want to be treated fairly by everyone all the time or else I am going to have a huge meltdown" is ridiculous.

Watch out for the "shoulds."
This is a way to trick yourself into being upset about things that you can't change. You can control yourself and your reactions, not others. If someone always greets you by calling you a fool, and you think they should not do this, you will be upset. You may as well wake up tomorrow and yell, "NOOOO! The sky is blue and I think it should be red!" It would be more accurate to say to yourself, or even the other person, "Oh, that's exactly what you should say to me, because that's usually what you say." However, the world is exactly the way it should be. Practice acceptance.

Don't keep it a secret.
Get help and don't be embarrassed to confer with friends or an adult. This is why people live together in groups. We are here to help each other. Many times I have met with a family who tells me the bullying went on for a long time before the child spoke out about it—especially children on the autism spectrum.

Throw them off balance by stepping towards them, making eye contact, and saying something really nice to them. Try these on for size: "Thanks for the feedback," or "I'll think about that," or "You would say that," or "I welcome the opportunity to demonstrate I can control myself." Smile and keep walking.

The student can also say, "Feel free to give me any criticism you want, because I've already decided nothing you can say can hurt or upset me." Remember, don't get upset, or at least don't show it. This makes you look like you are in control and makes the bully look more and more like a jerk if they continue.

Ask the student to list, check, or circle the strategies they are most comfortable trying. Explain that nothing works all the time, and if they try one strategy several times, it simply means it is time to try something else. This is how we solve problems—through effort, action, change, and experimentation.

When I was an elementary school counselor, I had a simple strategy that worked. I told the complaining target that he was going to have to confront the offending party in person in my office with me present to keep them safe. I taught and had them practice the "When you (call me stupid), I feel (mad), and I want you to (stop)." Sometimes if they seemed nervous, I had them write out the script for themselves. Typically, they don't really want to do this. I explained that I would then tell the other student that if I heard about the problem again, we would be having this meeting again in my office. Since this generally feels weird and awkward for them, they stop. I also got the targets to practice standing up for themselves, while teaching them a valuable skill and empowering them to deal with problems themselves and feel strong enough to handle it.

See how many wonderful teaching opportunities the gift of unfairness and criticism by others offers?

SCHOOL OR CLASSWIDE TECHNIQUES FOR BULLY PREVENTION

Teach what conflict is. Conflict can simply be a disagreement and is a normal part of relationships. Demonstrate how a conflict can be resolved without fireworks, such as yelling or fighting. "Let's play Chutes and Ladders!" "No, I really want to play checkers." "Okay, let's play checkers. Then if we have time, can we play my game?" "Sure." For more advanced students, teach the difference between the conflict styles of aggressive, passive-aggressive, submissive (victim), and assertive.

Train students in conflict resolution. For a simple list, see the document "Solve Your Own Problem." Emphasize the importance of a cooperative nature in groups, finding solutions that provide mutual benefits and de-emphasizing the need to win or be right. Provide a step-by-step concrete process for solving a problem.

Train peer mediators; there are many structured programs available out there for this. Have the student work in pairs and rotate the roles so they all get a chance to practice. Make this a first-through-twelfth-grade procedure.

ZINGERS AND COMEBACKS FOR VERBAL ABUSE AND PUT-DOWNS

- **You would say that.**
- **Wow, you really know how to hurt me.**
- **Does trying to hurt me make you feel better about yourself?**
- **If you put me down, do your so-called friends like you better?**
- **I'm sorry for you if your friends and parents talk to you that way.**
- **Okay, and by the way go ahead and offer whatever criticism you like, because I've already decided nothing you can say can hurt me.**
- **I know you are, but what am I?**
- **I'm rubber and you're glue; whatever you say bounces off of me and sticks to you.**

Remember, one of the ways we can make ourselves less of an easy target is to walk with a confident gait and appear switched on and aware of our surroundings.

I know, some of these possible responses are risky and may be controversial. It's a risky and controversial world we live in. I think you need to use your best judgment and discretion if you are coaching a child in ways to respond to bullying. Often the neurotypical kids are better at being sneaky and know how to provoke the kids on the spectrum, and the kid being bullied gets in trouble for retaliating. The whole crowded noisy public school scene doesn't work out well, anyway, for some kids with autism. You can also look for a small charter or private school.

— Chapter 5 —

EXECUTIVE FUNCTIONS

Executive functions, or executive skills, are brain skills. These brain skills originate from the frontal lobe of the brain, which is akin to the conductor of the orchestra of our behavior. This is the last part of the brain to develop in a fetus, so any disruption, such as premature birth, may result in this area of the brain failing to develop on the expected developmental timetable. You might say that milder disruptions in executive functions may result in ADHD, and more significant disruptions may result in autism spectrum disorder. It is also worthy to note that when a fetus turns male, a wash of testosterone kills many brain cells, which may explain why these type of symptoms manifest more often and more severely in male children. Some studies of human brains show that the neurons in the frontal lobe of neurotypical individuals are different in structure from other brain cells. However, in individuals with autism, the neurons in their

Do you have a child who seems smart but struggles to organize and regulate their behavior or emotions?

frontal lobe are the same as other neurons in the brain, or undifferentiated. In PET scans of people diagnosed with ADHD, there is little activity in the frontal lobe, while in people without ADHD, the amount of activity and energy use in the frontal lobe is much higher. Maybe that's why normal and routine or redundant activities are experienced as too boring and uncomfortable for the people with low frontal lobe activity; they need more novelty, risk, and excitement to pay attention.

Do you have a child who seems smart but struggles to organize and regulate their behavior or emotions?

WHY DOES THIS HAPPEN?

Often when children fail to meet our expectations we feel frustrated. For example, you ask your child to clean their room, and twenty minutes later you decide to check on his progress. You find there is none, as he is merely playing games in a dirty room. What gives? Or maybe you send your daughter to her room to put her shoes on. You tell her to meet you at the front door, as it is time to go to school. Fifteen minutes later you find her in her room fooling around with something interesting she found. Or how about the child who blows up when it is time to turn off the video game?

These children are often viewed as oppositional, defiant, or lazy. Actually, they are struggling because they lack the thinking skills to adapt successfully to changes in the environment or organize and regulate goal-directed behavior. These thinking skills are called executive functions.

When we ask a child to clean their room and they openly resist or obediently go to their room but don't get the job done, we often conclude they are unmotivated or defiant. We often fail to realize the child who is not getting the room picked up may lack the thinking skills nec-

> They are struggling because they lack the thinking skills to adapt successfully

essary to organize the task. They look at all the stuff in their room, and they don't know where to start. It's not that they won't or don't care, it's that they simply don't know how. The child who does not return to the front door with shoes on may have a weak working memory, again a thinking skill or executive function, and they forget what they are supposed to be doing. The child who blows up when it is time to turn off the video game may have weak skills in flexibility and emotional control.

The good news: these are teachable skills. What are they?

INHIBITION

This is the ability to filter inappropriate responses and not blurt them out or act on impulse.

WORKING MEMORY

This is short-term memory. The average person can hold seven bits (or chunks of information) within their short-term memory. There is a psychological link to why people can remember, at most, seven digits of a phone number. If working memory is not functioning well, then the information may not be held long enough to encode it into long-term memory. Thus, learning would be impaired. This is what is not working when you tell your kid to get his shoes on because it is time to go. Here is the typical scenario. He goes to his room but does not return soon after. You check on him and find him playing in his room. Your son's response is, "Oh yeah, I forgot."

METACOGNITION

This is the ability to think about what you are thinking about. Self-awareness is the product, and without it, we have a lack of ability to notice that what we are thinking is wrong or off-topic for the context. Individuals with weak metacognition may be unaware that they daydream even when you ask them. Have you ever asked, "What were you thinking?" and been given the answer of, "I don't know"? Here's your sign.

COGNITIVE FLEXIBILITY/SHIFT

This is the ability to shift mental sets. Most elementary school-age children who re-enter their classroom after recess activities are able to sit down quietly and engage in the next routine. However, some children continue to run, play, and shout. These are the ones who have failed to adjust their behavior to match the new context and continue to act as though they are still at recess. They are showing difficulty changing or shifting their mental set.

EMOTIONAL CONTROL

This is the ability to regulate behavior in the face of and tolerate strong emotions.

INITIATION

This is the ability to get started. Some people have difficulty beginning tasks, especially unpleasant or unpredictable ones, such as calling someone and making a social invitation. Some people overthink and overwhelm themselves. Ready, shoot, aim.

SUSTAIN ATTENTION

This is the ability to maintain attention and not become distracted. Squirrel!

ORGANIZATION

Organization is about the ability to put things into categories and break larger tasks into more manageable steps. We do this while cleaning a desk or room. Some folks take one look at the mess and don't know where to start; they tend to get lost in all of the details.

PRIORITIZATION

The person who spends so much time choosing a font for their project that they don't get it written in the allotted time is showing trouble with prioritization.

PLANNING

This is the ability to think about the future. The person with this capacity is ready when it's time to go and can use a calendar to schedule events.

NEUROPLASTICITY: HOW THE BRAIN CHANGES ITSELF

The good news is that if some part of the brain is damaged or fails to develop as expected, another part, with practice and effort, grows to manage a task with ever-increasing fluency. When someone has a stroke, they may become hemiplegic—unable to move half of their body. The part of the brain that controlled that half of the body is dead, never to return again. Imagine that your grandmother's physical therapist visits her in her home or hospital room to begin rehabilitation exercises. After only one attempt, the therapist tells you, "Nope, she didn't want to work at it and couldn't do it. I guess we're done here. No way." However, the therapist decides to try one more time by pushing, cajoling, and encouraging her. With any luck, grandma will go from a wheelchair to a walker to a cane. Hopefully, after months of work, she will again be able to walk independently and speak clearly again. This is because some other area of her brain took over that function and organized itself and grew until the behavior/movement could be performed with greater fluency. We can do the same with all kinds of thinking and behavior skills. Practice, practice, reward, and practice. Never give up. That's what makes this kind of intervention a hard sell; it's a lot of repetitive work, and none too exciting.

> Far too often they are judged and criticized as being lazy, oppositional, lacking discipline, or morally defective.

I think that executive skills remediation tends to be overlooked as an intervention. These are thinking skills that we can compensate for. When we teach the expected behaviors, but an individual doesn't have the underlying processing hardware available (the thinking skills), they still fall short of doing what they know is expected and have trouble keeping up.

> Folks, we have to stop this.

Far too often they are judged and criticized as being lazy, oppositional, lacking discipline, or morally defective. Folks, we have to stop this. I can't begin to tell you how many people I've seen who suffered through their adult life because of the way they were inaccurately labeled and treated in childhood. I believe there are many cases where it is not a person's autism, or ADHD, or dyslexia, or whatever, that makes them "sick," creating low self-esteem, or anger, or depression, anxiety, and so on.

It is within an environment whereby they are repeatedly being asked to do something that makes them feel ill. The way in which they are being treated by others is what is making them sick.

EXECUTIVE FUNCTION REMEDIATION/ COMPENSATION STRATEGIES

In general, we need to teach the appropriate skills. Keep in mind the concept of plasticity, which is the brain's ability, through effort, positive reinforcement, and coaching to form new connections and even generate new neurons to create capabilities that are not currently present. A good example of what happens in any kind of therapy is the stroke patient who loses the ability to move half of her body due to damage in the brain. In physical therapy, she is encouraged to work and move and she progresses from the wheelchair to a walker to a cane to walking unassisted. New parts of the brain can develop and assume functions with time and effort (*The Brain That Changes Itself*, by Norman Doidge, MD, 2007).

Observation. Watch for situations and specific information about when they are successful and when they are not. Modify tasks to match current abilities. For example, ask them to study for only fifteen minutes, if that is how long they can perform the task before becoming distracted.

Use Incentives. Set the person up with first, then scenarios to gradually build skills. Suggest to them that they first plan their homework schedule or study for seventeen minutes and then call their friends to ask if they would like to play Frisbee in the park.

Set up practice trials.

Provide only as much support as needed.

Gradually remove supports and scaffolding.

Be aware that the first skills to go when under stress are the weakest "links." Make a plan for the person to manage stress, exercise often, sleep regular hours, and take a brief nap in the day if they can. They can schedule fun and "down" time but should avoid late-night parties.

MODIFY THE ENVIRONMENT. REMEMBER THE ABC'S.

Antecedent.

This is what comes before the behavior. For example, if you notice that when your child stays up late and the following morning he is more distracted than usual, set an earlier bedtime for him. If your child seems to focus better after exercising, then suggest that he exercise before tackling homework. Create a regular time and place to plan and study. Set alarms or appointment reminders on the phone or computer to support self-monitoring and staying on schedule. Notice if your child studies best while sitting up, lying down, on the bed, on the floor, with the TV on or off, in a public or private place, with natural or artificial lighting, and/or with or without a snack.

Behavior.

What you watch to determine if your plan is working.

Consequence.

Manipulate what comes after successful efforts to reward.

Inhibit.

Practice and reward not giving in to impulses such as interruptions or responding to provocations from siblings or peers. Build the skill. For young children, make them earn things so they learn to delay gratification. Help them to understand there are consequences (natural or supplied by you) for poor self-control. Prepare them for situations requiring them to wait; practice role-play.

Working memory.

Make lists and activity schedules, send text messages, create picture boards, practice saying digits backwards, take notes, draw pictures symbolizing intentions and concepts, and teach rehearsal (subvocalizing) and memorization strategies. Utilize a smart phone or day planner, as well as a vibrating alarm. Have a child repeat over and over in a chant or sing-song as they are embarking on a task, "Go to my room, find my shoes, put them on, and go to the front door." Practice daily repeating digits, starting where they are fluent. You can say to them something like, "I'm going to say some numbers, and I want you to say them back to me: 3, 4, 9." When they get good at repeating seven digits, start back at two or three but have them say the digits back to you backwards (9, 4, 3). Go to intensivecareforyou.com and look on the *Resources for Free* page for the document "Working Memory Remediation," and you will find a list of numerals for you to use with instructions.

Emotional control.

The Incredible 5-point Scale, by Buron and Curtis, 1993, teaches us how to grade and build earlier awareness that an emotional response is occurring. Suggest relaxation strategies, such as meditation. Activity tools include doing anything fun, exercising, or engaging in social situations (talking to someone they trust). Thinking tools involve grading the size of the problem on a scale from 1–10. Systematic desensitization works by imagining the feared outcome and then practicing relaxation to train the body to relax in the face of stressful stimuli. Make a chart that includes the following: triggers to angry or worried feelings; activities the person may want to do but can't; good things to do with upset feelings; how to be mad the right way; and what to do or think to help themselves feel better. Then practice daily in role-play. Remind and reward generously when triggers occur. This encourages practice "in real life."

Sustained attention.

Set up a visual time-timer (www.timetimer.com) or self-monitoring tape (www.addwarehouse.com). Time-timer.com also has programmable vibrating watch alarms you can set at irregular intervals to remind you to check if you are on task. It also describes incentives, praise, reducing distractions, following a schedule and creating a space for homework, as well as healthy breaks.

Task initiation.

Just do the first problem (trick yourself into starting, then you may do one more). Emphasize the importance of doing it now instead of later, offer visual cues, reinforce for timeliness, set alarms, have the child make a schedule and define how cues will be given, make a list and prioritize it, and get a coach to text several times a week to monitor progress.

Planning/prioritization.

In this person-centered plan, you can do the following: break tasks into smaller steps; help the child make a schedule; use things they really want as rewards when steps are completed; schedule planning time daily as well as times to check progress on the plan and mark out completed tasks; and get a buddy to talk it out with and take notes.

Organization.

Put a system in place and monitor it for fidelity. Do the following: make labels or pictures to show what goes where; draw pictures of how it should look; make a space for everything that is clearly marked; and schedule a time to organize. Also, make a checklist for routines and the steps for cleaning a room. The child can interact with this by checking off steps or moving pictures of steps arranged in sequence from a "now" position to a "done" box.

Time management.

Use schedules, calendars, and alarms www.watchminder.com. Write down estimates of how long each step in a task will take. Record results to learn whether you'll need to adjust the duration of certain activities. Schedule and plan for breaks and minimize distractions.

Flexibility.

Learn to watch out for absolute or extreme forms of thinking errors and correct the thoughts. Keep an eye out for words in self-talk such as never, always, have to, and can't. Make a game with extreme statements such as, "I always miss," "I never get it right," or "You never let me do anything" made by a person when a disappointing or unexpected event occurs. Have the child generate smarter and more accurate self-talk such as, "I missed this time, but if I keep trying, I will get it."

Metacognition.

Teach your child to ask himself questions such as, "What am I thinking about," "Is what I am doing working," "What is another way to do this," and "How do I know when I am finished." Have the child keep a journal of thoughts that distract him or occur when he is having an emotional response. Prompt the child to evaluate their own performance. Ask them, "How do you think you did?" Ask them to predict how their actions may make others feel. Teach them to listen first and use comments to find out more about others, rather than lecturing or correcting others. Practice these at the dinner table.

Goal-directed persistence.

Start out with easy items and build up gradually. Use tasks the child enjoys, such as increasingly difficult Lego building projects. Chart progress so they can see how they are getting better at working longer. Allow them to earn money for chores and set up a savings program for something big they really want.

Self-awareness/other-awareness.

Using video, play back to the student and help them identify all the things they did well in terms of prosocial behavior and effective communication. Then, help them pick one thing they would like to work on during the next video. This interaction can be amongst peers or with a coach, such as in Interpersonal Recall Therapy conducted by some speech pathologists. Use video and pause on frames that hold an expression on another's face and ask the following questions: "What could this mean," "What is this person thinking," "Who are they having these thoughts about," and "What could be the consequences for you if you continue this behavior." Develop a self-monitoring sheet with numerous boxes for different times during the day. Have the student place a checkmark on the sheet if they are on task or an "x" if they are not. Provide graduated rewards, based not on the number of times on task but on the number of times they noticed if they were or were not on task.

Keep in mind that if inhibition or working memory are poorly developed, these must be targeted first, as subsequent organizational and self-control strategies are unlikely to take root until these are addressed.

Try Googling "Mind Up" to see the executive skills curriculum that has been legislated as mandatory for public schools in several states. Google "Tools of the Mind" to see research and techniques involving an executive skills curriculum. This has been piloted in many school districts with huge successes. The kids who were enrolled in the executive skills curriculum rather than the academic curriculum dramatically outperformed their control group peers in the standardized academic testing at the end of their school years.

This is part of what makes socializing so difficult. We need to think about what we want to say as well as consider what others are saying to us. We also need to watch their reactions to us—all at the same time!

Chapter 6

COMMUNICATION

What makes this so tricky?

Thinking in pictures versus thinking in words.

When I'm doing a live workshop I like to ask people, "What are your thoughts?" Then I get more specific by asking, "I mean, are your thoughts of pictures or words? When you think, is it like a movie in your mind, or more like a feeling you get? Or, do you hear talking inside your head? If so, whose voice is it?" Do you have conversations with other people in your head, and when you think, do you combine this with feelings and images? If you are thinking in pictures or a video stream, how do you step outside your video to make another video to analyze the first video? In other words, how do you think about what you are "thinking" about to analyze how reasonable your thoughts are? Also, are you thinking about what you intend to think about or are supposed to think about? If you are thinking in words, you can think to yourself, *That makes me mad; I'd like to kick her—*

whoops, no, I better not, that would be mean, and I could get in trouble. Voila! We have self-monitor and inhibition skills!

Language, in the form of words, makes this possible; words are a shortcut. If I am thinking in words, it's easy for me to say those words to someone else, and they will probably understand what I am trying to convey with the words. But I can't upload a video from my head to yours. Remember those primitive TRS80 computers that came out in the early 80s? One of the first games, *Gilgamesh's Tavern*, was constructed with scripts, or words running down the screen. Then we started playing games with more graphics, and we needed a LOT more processing power and memory. It may be like this for our brains, too. Thinking in words only uses a little capacity, while thinking in pictures or graphics takes a lot more. Words are a shortcut that bridge understanding from me to you. What if I were trying to communicate to you with pictures and we didn't share a common lexicon? I can't plug in to you and download my internal video stream.

Engineers tend to describe themselves as picture-thinkers, while teachers will tell you that they are word-thinkers. When a word-thinker learns that there are those who think not in words, but in pictures, they often are flabbergasted and are taken aback. They have a difficult time bending their mind around this alien thought form.

An engineer can look at something and instantly grasp how it works or how to put it together. What happens when they try to explain it? They get frustrated because it's so obvious to them that it is right there in plain sight, but finding the words for the picture-thinker to explain it to the word-thinker is a daunting task. It's like the two different languages of the Mac and the PC.

We use self-talk, or inner language, to regulate emotions and problem solve. Teaching self-talk skills is critical to developing more efficient and effective communication, emotional regulation, and problem-solving skills.

This is why I encourage the use of visual supports; they don't need to be fancy. You can draw stick figures with thought and word bubbles to convey a message about social expectations and outcomes. This is quite helpful to people on the spectrum because of their difficulty forming the concepts that words

Teaching self-talk skills is critical to developing more efficient and effective communication

are meant to represent. Add a visual to help build understanding and use it as a prompt or reminder again later in a teachable moment. When we see repetitive behaviors, this often signals that the child's brain is unable to assimilate the perceptual patterns into a meaningful whole, and so they are stuck repeating. This also explains how some kids can repeat the sound patterns of a passage they read or a video they heard but are unable to answer comprehension questions about what they have memorized. They have the pattern but not the concepts that are symbolized. Also, when they are in an environment that becomes non-meaningful, they may engage in repetitive and even disruptive behaviors, such as shrieking. They are trying to create a pattern they know to drown out the nonsense, which could be the background noise of other people quietly talking or possibly an air conditioner running.

How do you teach someone to begin using their inner language to self-regulate and problem-solve, to become a more fluent user of word-based language? You can narrate what they are doing as they do it by saying, "Oh, now you are trying to make the blue one balance on top of the yellow block." You can narrate your own experience and do your thinking out loud by stating, "Hmm, well, this key is not unlocking the door. I could try and force it, but it might break. Let me try one of the other keys to see if it works better." Finally, get the child to restate a word problem out loud in their own words and talk their way out loud through possible paths to solutions. "So, you have eleven apples to start, and you take away three because two are given away and you eat one, so…that would be like eleven minus three. I'm supposed to say how many are left—that would be eight apples left."

Pragmatics is the use of language in social situations. A person can have a highly developed vocabulary and still not communicate effectively with others. Social skills groups and speech therapy in small groups can help.

> Research indicates that only 7 percent of a person's message is communicated by the words they say; the other 93 percent of the message is conveyed by nonverbal cues

Research indicates that only 7 percent of a person's message is communicated by the words they say; the other 93 percent of the message is conveyed by nonverbal cues such as tone, expression, and body posture. Try playing charade games that require the use and interpretation of nonverbal communication only. There are several Cranium games that incorporate charades, sculpting, and drawing to guess a word, such as Cranium Conga. This is perfect, because it is a "guess what I am thinking" game, which is exactly what we want our kids to be in the habit of doing when they share space with others—to monitor them closely at all times for mostly nonverbal clues—about what they are thinking and planning.

— Chapter 7 —

SENSORY ISSUES

Many people with autism have trouble organizing sensory input into meaningful categories and packets. Proprioception is how you determine where you are in relation to other objects, such as the wall, the floor, and other people. If you are seated right now, your brain coordinates and makes sense of what you feel through your seat, your feet, and your back. It takes in information about balance from your inner ear and gathers data from your eyes to help you know you are safely seated—not too close or too far relative to others. Your brain is making sure you are safe and not at risk of falling. Someone with disrupted proprioception either isn't getting all the sensory data into their brain or their brain isn't making consistent sense of the data for the individual to know they are safe and not at risk of falling. Consequently, this person may start seeking more information by bouncing in their seat to move more data to their brains from their backsides. They may also touch the floor or others around them or sit on one leg since this compresses the knee joint which is full of nerve endings.

Many people with autism have trouble organizing sensory input into meaningful categories and packets

When seated on the floor, some of these children may roll around and touch others repeatedly after being prompted to sit still and keep their hands to themself. When walking down the hall they drag a hand along the wall. If you make them withdraw the hand, they have trouble walking in a straight line and may zigzag from wall to wall. This is because their balance and vision are not developed enough to keep them oriented to the correct distance from other people and the right-side wall in the hall. Some kids with sensory issues may start getting anxious about going to school, not be able to communicate why, and even refuse to go. Others may act out at school or arrive home hyperactive and begin to crash around as a result of sensory disintegration and overload.

What do you do? Put them in a beanbag chair or seat them on a deep soft cushion or put a lap weight or weighted vest on them. Send them out for some running around and joint compressions. You might try brushing therapy with the Wilbarger Protocol (Google it if you are not familiar with this technique). Send them for occupational therapy to remediate the problem as much as possible. You can schedule breaks in the school day for downtime. Some schools have an Occupational Therapy (OT) sensory room. I've seen children taking their breaks in one of these rooms; they receive the kind of sensory input they need to become organized and focused again. Sometimes we can prevent the overload and acting out by scheduling sensory activities like swinging or jumping at regular times during the day. We call this a "sensory diet." We can also assign at these regular intervals what are known as "heavy work activities." You can see several lists of these posted in the *Resources for Free* page at www.intensivecareforyou.com.

Another effective intervention is to find out what is unpleasant and overwhelming and avoid the trigger, like warning them about upcoming triggers beforehand, or keeping them out of fire drills. It can be hard to know when to push a kid to get them used to something and when to relent.

One time I was in an ARD/IEP meeting for an elementary student who had not eaten his lunch in six months because the noise in the cafeteria was just too much for him. The principal said, "Well, he's got to learn to get used to the cafeteria sometime." Really? How has not eating lunch impacted the child's learning, physical, and mental health? I don't eat in cafeterias because I don't like them; this has not caused me any problems. There's nothing wrong with accommodating the student and letting them eat somewhere else. It is not essential for a child to be comfortable in a cafeteria because this is not a skill necessary to become an independent and productive member of society.

> We can prevent the overload and acting out by scheduling sensory activities like swinging or jumping at regular times during the day. We call this a "sensory diet."

FUNCTIONAL IMPLICATIONS: DISRUPTED SENSORY PROCESSING

How overwhelming is a kinder room? With all of the noise, the number of people, and all of the stuff on the walls, where can they go to escape and recharge? I would suggest that a reasonable accommodation would be to provide a couple of breaks during the day in a very low-stimulation environment. Here you can cut out some windows in a dishwasher box and let the student decorate it as a private "office" where they can crash on a beanbag chair and wrap up in a snuggly blanket. Some people are unable to eat in a noisy, crowded cafeteria. Does a student mostly get into trouble while in music class? Put a chair or desk just outside the room where they can get away but still be seen. Or, give them some earplugs, headphones, or earmuffs. It can be hard to know when to push a kid to get them used to something and when to relent, but in a situation where they are not eating lunch for months or they are becoming aggressive, I think the answer should be crystal clear. Let them eat someplace else.

Chapter 8

STUDENT INTERVIEWS:

What Was Hard and What Helped?

I interviewed a couple of students who had significant difficulty in academia (beginning with kindergarten) and who eventually found themselves finding friends, fitting in, and doing well in school without further outbursts or disciplinary removals.

When I interviewed these students, they identified stress and fitting in with peers as the two most important factors to manage in achieving success and a modicum of comfort in both school and life.

The following is a list of what they said they had trouble with and what helped.

WHAT WAS HARD

- Trouble being with so many kids in one classroom.
- Trouble staying on topic.
- People said I was gay in third grade.
- Trouble starting conversations.
- Asking too many questions and then being shut out.
- Correcting others so often I get ignored or told to mind my own business. (I bet they get corrected often, and so they think that's how to interact!)
- Getting bullied—even in kindergarten—and the teacher didn't help.
- Can't remember names.
- I have no idea why I get picked on so much.
- I get stressed out easily.
- Special education teachers focus too much on the disorder and what's wrong.

WHAT HELPED

- I need a place to hide or get away from everybody for a while.
- Learning not to stay stuck on injustices.
- I made a commitment to not be miserable this year; I wound up making a few friends.
- Finding ways to let stress out.
- Engaging in pleasurable activities.

- **Earplugs.**

- **Unschool: taking a break from school for a year.**

- **Testing for learning style and matching learning activities.**

CONCLUDING COMMENTS (WHAT THEY SAID)

Here is what some of my young clients on the spectrum said:

"Remember, they are people too—people who are a little different—but not all that different from you."

"Consider modifying their environment to help them avoid stress and meet their needs."

"Focus on interests and learning and developing a passion rather than taking a test. Don't make it all just work, work, work."

"I hope nobody has to go through what I did. Everyone should have someone they can rely on, that they can trust." Find them someone at school they can rely on and trust.

"Medicines may have side effects."

They identified stress and fitting in with peers as the two most important factors to manage in achieving success

WHAT WOULD YOUR IDEAL SCHOOL LOOK LIKE?

"You would have a quiet place to get away from everyone and take a break. More opportunities for movement. Less paper and pencil tasks, worksheets, and no homework. If there is something you are interested in, your teacher would act as a guide, helping you research and learn. Then you could present your findings to the class."

Chapter 9

SELF-ESTEEM

Finding your power to build it back up

How often do they get ranked at the bottom socially or in academics? How often do they receive negative or corrective feedback versus praise and support?

Praising for how smart they are has pitfalls, such as avoidance of any tasks in which they may not excel. Instead, attempt to praise the characteristics of perseverance and grit. Wanting to be the best every time can create dis-ease within the self when that lofty goal doesn't materialize. Therefore, you should focus on praising reasonable effort and perseverance.

Recent research on self-esteem indicates that a lot of our satisfaction or lack thereof comes from ranking. We constantly are comparing ourselves to others, so encourage them to become really good at something. You can provide them with private lessons and create practice opportunities for something they have passion and talent for.

I hope you had at least one person you knew growing up who influenced you to think of yourself in positive and encouraging ways. In middle school I had an English teacher, Billie Hoffman, whose eyes crinkled and twinkled smilingly even when someone displayed inappropriate behavior. One time she overheard a classmate use a word that doesn't belong in the classroom. She grinned and had the student pull his chair up to her desk. As she smiled even more broadly (as always), she said to him, as well as the other students who were within earshot, "Why don't you tell us what you think that word means, Bob?" She could always defuse and redirect with her quiet humor and ever-smiling face. She never needed to get mad, show frustration, offer criticism, or judge. Somehow just knowing that she could see you and know that you possessed goodness and the capacity to do better made her able to handle any sort of problem in her classroom. She had mastered the art of something very valuable; she learned to *see what the kids could be, not just what they are not.* What sort of contributions might their uniqueness create? Billie Hoffman never lowered herself to use fear, threats, or the pain of punishment to maintain order in our space.

Along the way, there were a few others who inspired me to become my best self. These were all people who loved the power of love more than they loved power itself.

My intention with this paragraph is to give you permission to become the person who can influence another with the power of love, encouragement, and positivity, as did the few great masters who influenced me. Be wary of looking at a person as a problem to be solved. Children want an opportunity to engage in making the world; they are made stronger when their voices and abilities are recognized.

Chapter 10

TUNNEL VISION

Trouble seeing the forest through the trees?

Preoccupation with details and lacking central coherence and the ability to comprehend the big picture can be a problematic characteristic of autism. Frequent reminders to step back and ask "What is this really about," and "What does this person want from me" can make this kind of thinking more automatic. Developing special interests may help create an experience of central coherence and help develop an identity. How would you feel driving into a city where every single billboard called your name, and you had to read each and every word on those signs? Wouldn't you rather have a brain that can easily detach from non-salient details and can stay focused on what is relevant to your intentions and safety?

Chapter 11

SOCIAL SKILLS

The Key to a Happy Life

Difficulty reading the context and knowing how rules change with different places and people can interfere with social success. Remember, they are little and still developing. Consider their media consumption—what if they imitate what they are absorbing? An aggressive style of dealing with conflict is a common characteristic of video games and television. Some kids are just better off not being exposed to the fear-pandering news media and frightening or aggressive viewing content. Garbage in, garbage out. Please carefully monitor and manage what is going into your child's brain.

Social skills take time and effort to develop, which is why I have a video solely devoted to teaching social skills to children aged 4–8 (a great video course at www.intensivecareforyouvideo.com). In the *Resources* section at the end of this book, you will find a thorough list containing: games, books, and curricula that I have found useful in my practice conducting social skills groups over the past fifteen years.

These are the most important things I learned about social skills:

You have to get buy-in.

This means you must create an experience in which it is more fun and exciting being in the group than it is to be alone. If you have a person who doesn't want to be in the group and doesn't want to work on social skills, your job is going to be much more difficult.

Birds of a feather flock together.

A child who is spectrum-ish may do better and feel more comfortable befriending other children who are quirky in similar ways. Think *Big Bang Theory*.

Some kids are just better off not being exposed to the fear-pandering news media and frightening or aggressive viewing content

All the social skills work and therapy in the world may not result in making someone who stands out as being a little different blend in perfectly with neurotypicals. Instead, target embracing the differences and celebrating strengths. When a person is comfortable with themselves, can acknowledge and laugh about their idiosyncrasies, and doesn't get all nervous and weird about themselves in a group, they can be found by others as very likable and personable. Having these capabilities is more important in relationships than exhibiting perfect social skills.

Chapter 12

PROBLEM SOLVING

Getting unstuck

Having trouble recognizing there may be many ways to solve the same problem, the autistic brain may try one particular method and then have difficulty adapting and attempting another strategy if unsuccessful. It may get stuck or fall apart here and tend not to use internal dialogue or self-talk to problem solve. We can teach talking out and generating multiple solutions through narration and modeling; narrate their efforts, and think out loud in their presence when you are solving a problem.

Use the "problem-solving template" in the *Resources for Free* page at my site to reinforce the idea that there are many possible solutions to try for the same problem.

They may exhibit "Frank Sinatra syndrome" (I want it my way) regarding all interpersonal problems, or at least especially when they

The autistic brain may try one particular method and then have difficulty adapting and attempting another strategy if unsuccessful

become emotionally involved. One of the things that autistic brains have trouble with is inhibiting a previously learned pattern. When someone keeps getting stuck with the wrong response in a particular situation, try representing it visually, like using a comic strip type conversation, showing the thoughts and feelings of characters and representing the more adaptive way for the person to respond, not just in words but with visual support also.

— Chapter 13 —

PERSEVERATION STATION

Perseveration (pər-se-və-rā-shən) becomes a problem when it interferes with normal life activities, especially when someone becomes "caught in a loop," and that circle involves escalating emotions. The target of the perseveration may be about a past emotional injury, such as bullying, teasing, an injustice, or possibly a fear about the future ("What if…"). It also could be about something the person wants to do or have that is not possible or reasonable to obtain at that particular moment. The person may believe they must "do" or "have" something in particular. Then they emotionally escalate and even become aggressive in the attempt to get or do something they want in order to satisfy their anxiety about getting or not getting.

There are several ways to help someone overcome a perseverative behavior or verbalization. One method is to abruptly interrupt or redirect, by either quickly substituting a safer topic to think about or suggesting an activity or providing an object as a distraction.

A second option would be to gently redirect by joining in and mirroring the perseverative behavior and modifying it slightly to make it a socially relevant conversation or game.

You could also try a cognitive-behavioral technique by exploring the logical problem with thinking you "must" or you "have to." This is a good time to review those things we actually must have to survive, like air and water. Point out the differences between "wanting" and "needing" as well as between "want to" and "have to."

Remind them to "Catch the thought" and "Use your brain filter." State that not all thoughts need to be spoken and ask them to consider what others want and need to hear from them.

Make a T-chart of both good and not so good things to think about.

Explain the process and problem of "getting stuck in a loop" and generate a catch phrase to cue the person to make an effort to think and talk about one of their good things to think about. You could also use a gesture such as placing your hand over your mouth and saying "Oops! Catch yourself!"

Explore with your subject how they feel when they get stuck. Do you like this feeling? How do you know when you are getting stuck? How do people around you think and feel when you repeat the same thing over and over? Do other people like you better when you pay attention to what they are talking about?

Behaviorally, you could ignore the person and move away from them when the perseveration presents. Then offer rewards when the person successfully catches themselves and stops or switches to something else.

If the perseveration has an obsessive-compulsive component, you could practice Exposure and Response Prevention (ERP) with the help of a professional counselor or psychologist. For example, your subject gets stuck thinking they must get up and open and close the door seven times. You would spend several minutes a day asking them to think really hard for several minutes about having to do this behavior, and then don't allow them to do it. Continue this for two to four weeks. If one disruptive behavior stops and other ones appear, you can switch to another obsession/compulsion.

Finally, you could make a "Perseveration Station" for the stuck person to visit. This is a place that has highly desired activities that are incompatible with the perseveration—hopefully, interesting enough to engage and distract. Or, you could direct them to this place at a regularly scheduled time of day and instruct them to spend fifteen minutes perseverating (per-se-ver-at-ing), hoping that they will get tired of it and say, "But I don't want to do this anymore," or "I don't want to worry." This would be practicing paradoxical intention.

— Chapter 14 —

COMORBID MOOD DISORDERS

Could there be something going on along with autism symptoms? If someone has more than one mental condition at the same time, they are said to have "comorbid conditions."

About 65 percent of people with autism spectrum disorder have a comorbid mood disorder according to Tony Attwood, a world-recognized Aspergers authority; so it's more the rule than the exception. Counseling, behavior therapy, psychoeducation, and medication are possible avenues for relief. Psychoeducation means teaching the person diagnosed about their condition and suggesting what they can do to manage it. Psychoeducation includes attending workshops, conducting research on the internet, watching videos, or engaging in bibliotherapy, which means reading books to educate. I think it is empowering when you can motivate someone to do their own research. They need to, personally, experiment with varying solutions to their emotional and behavioral difficulties.

WHY IS THIS IMPORTANT TO KNOW?

Be ready to seek help if needed in treating concurrent mental health issues if they develop. Any mention of killing themselves should receive immediate professional attention. When a family physician or neurologist is treating with medication, they often prefer to refer the person to a psychiatrist for the more complex medication issues.

About 65 percent of people with autism spectrum disorder have a comorbid mood disorder

Chapter 15

EXTREME EMOTIONAL RESPONSE

Emotional responses may be either excessive or lacking. Typically, a child with autism spectrum disorder may be three years behind in emotional development, so if an eight-year-old throws tantrums like a five-year-old, this is not unexpected. They may tend not to grade feelings or distinguish a range and gradation of feelings—either calm or top-of-the-scale angry. It may seem like they are either happy or full-tilt angry, with nothing in between.

If they are having major meltdowns daily or several times per week, I suggest dramatically cutting back adult demands until they return to their emotional baseline. Teach them skills for frustration tolerance, build self-esteem through success, and then gradually add the work demands back in. An example would be giving a reward for simply attending school without becoming disruptive. At first, don't give them any work requirements; then slowly add some work requests as part of how they earn their rewards.

Help them develop an emotional vocabulary; use numbers and pictures to represent levels of intensity for the emotion. For example: 1 = calm, 2 = annoyed, 3 = frustrated, 4 = mad, and 5 = furious. Have them draw their own pictures or faces to go with the levels. I've also used animals and weather patterns for this practice. For example: 1 = a sunny day, 2 = a cloudy day, 3 = rain, 4 = storm, and 5 = tornado. To see this process in greater detail, refer to my video course, Anger and Children and/or Anxiety and Children at www.intensivecareforyouvideo.com.

> It may seem like they are either happy or full-tilt angry, with nothing in between

I think it's important for people to both recognize and convey their feelings, and the end result is definitely more beneficial when these are expressed in words rather than behavior! A person who is exhibiting emotional excess needs to know not only what they can't do, but what they can do when upset. They need a way to signal or communicate when they require assistance, a break, or use of a coping skill.

Brenda Smith Myles came up with a clever way to facilitate this process—the power card. I've used these cards in my practice. First, they pick a favorite hero, and then we select an image on the computer and print it out pocket-sized. On the back of this card we add a social story about what the hero does when he is angry. Then the kids can show their card to signal when they are upset and need a break or a distraction. Here's an example of what an eight-year-old made in a social skills group about his superhero Hawkeye:

When Hawkeye is hanging out with other people at home or in the community, people sometimes say things that he doesn't like. They might tell him "No," or say something a little mean or hurtful. Usually other people are not trying to hurt anybody's feelings. When Hawkeye is upset, at first he may want to run away or pierce them with an arrow, but that would be an overreaction that would surprise, confuse, or even scare other people. Hawkeye knows he needs to have a small reaction to small problems and use his words to say how he feels and ask for what he wants, like, "That bothers me; I wish you would (You fill in the blank)."

Hawkeye has a hard time controlling his reactions and he will try to use his words and not yell, run away, or shoot people for saying things he doesn't like. Then other people will know how he feels and what he wants, and they will feel more comfortable being around him.

Chapter 16

TEACHING RESPONSIBILITY AND INDEPENDENCE:

Telling Versus Asking

If you're looking for a life hack on how to be a good parent, this is it. Find out why this is both good news and bad news!

The moral of the story here is: Don't be the genius! As long as you keep giving the answers and telling kids what they should do, you run the risk that they will not learn to rely on themselves to solve their own problems and make decisions.

Let's say you've got <u>an angry escalating kid</u> on your hands. Here are some response choices:

Why don't you go to your room and cool off?	**What do you think you will do?**
You shouldn't be so angry.	**Why are you mad?**
Don't yell.	**How can you calm yourself?**
Stop it.	**Do you want to try any of your coping strategies to help yourself feel better now?**

What's the difference? In the left-hand column, who is taking responsibility for fixing feelings and problems? What is going to happen if the child thinks the parent or helping adult is responsible for fixing their problems and feelings? Might they target that caregiver and try to make the caregiver make them okay? Maybe they will attempt to bully and intimidate until their feelings subside or the caregiver takes some action that gets the child what they want? If you take responsibility for making them okay, they may begin to blame you whenever they are not. Yet it may seem that nothing you tell them makes them okay.

As long as you keep giving the answers and telling kids what they should do, you run the risk that they will not learn to rely on themselves

In the right-hand column (the responsibility for action), resolution is placed on the person experiencing a problem or emotional response. They are empowered to find and believe that they can figure it out, that they and only they are responsible for what they feel and do. Which do you prefer?

GETTING READY FOR SCHOOL

Get dressed; we have to leave soon.	I am noticing that you are not dressed and we are leaving in fifteen minutes.
Get dressed now!	What is your plan?
How many times do I have to tell you?	What do you need to do to be ready for school? The next step would be, after a few days, to look at them and wait a moment before heading out the door to see if they can initiate proper action on their own.

CLEANING AND CHORES

Put your dishes in the dishwasher.	What did we decide would happen if you don't put your dishes in the dishwasher?

By asking questions rather than telling answers, an adult can guide the child toward performing the work—*the noticing and the thinking, themselves*. They need to believe they can and that it's up to them. They can decide. They can figure it out. They have the internal resources to manage their feelings and problems. Are you interested in a quick solution to the problem now, or long-term learning and growing in independence and personal responsibility? Ask them the questions they need to be asking for themselves.

SELF-ASSESSMENT

Place a check next to the sentences that are true for you.

- ❑ **I keep telling them what they should do and to use their coping skills, but they won't listen.**

- ❑ **I express confidence that they can figure it out. I offer empathy and support. I reflect so they know I understand what they think and feel.**

- ❑ **I remain frustrated that nothing I tell them works.**

- ❑ **It's my fault they are upset. It's my job to make them feel better and make the world better for them.**

- ❑ **Only they can create and resolve their own feelings.**

- ❑ **I can't stand it when they are angry or upset.**

- ❑ **I can remain calm and supportive without enabling or blaming when they are angry or upset.**

- ❑ **I am responsible for what they do and feel.**

- ❑ **They don't do what I tell them to do, and I have to tell them over and over again.**

- ❑ **I have to do all the noticing and reminding. Then I become resentful and start to nag, and they tune me out even more. I do all the thinking for them; their brain is in neutral or already checked out.**

If you ask, they can start thinking and noticing for themselves. They are responsible for themselves and their actions.

What is a victim mindset? Would you say that they make you get angry and yell?

Could you be placing yourself in a martyr mindset? What does this mean?

There's no scorekeeping here—just food for thought.

How does this relate to everyday entitlement and narcissism?

How do you model for them? Do you take responsibility for your own actions and feelings, or do you blame them? Do you ally yourself with them and join in with blaming the teacher, the school, or the sibling?

Do you like to be told what to do? Are you in the habit of telling others what to do? This behavior does not foster healthy communication; it tears relationships apart.

If you always try to protect them from the realities and injustices, what are you teaching? That they can't take care of themselves? That the world should be fair? That they are always dependent on you to fix things for them?

If you keep them comfortable, rather than allow them to be uncomfortable, you are removing their motivation to try something new, to grow and change. We grow and change when we are uncomfortable; it's the challenge that spurs us toward new and greater efforts. If we are perfectly comfortable and cared for, why do the work and why bother to change?

By asking rather than telling, we are not merely teaching responsibility. We are demonstrating respect and trust and fostering confidence and self-esteem, while connecting and building our relationships. We are showing faith that the child can notice problems and solve them on their own.

Remember that what your kids want most from you is your appreciation and to feel they are important.

If you had planted seeds and were disappointed by their lack of growth or slow growth, you wouldn't withhold water to teach them a lesson and make them grow faster and stronger, right? So it is with children and your heartfelt appreciation and praise.

— Chapter 17 —

DEFENSE MECHANISMS

These defense mechanisms illustrate the importance of treating someone who is struggling with support, encouragement, and compassion. Feeling rejected, judged, and criticized engenders tendencies to rebel and resist or withdraw and give up.

Denial and always right/never wrong: In this God mode, the person may misinterpret the intentions of others. For instance, if the person has lost at a game, it was because someone cheated or made them lose on purpose as an act of aggression or righteous indignation. These people tend to make good lawyers. They have compelling arguments that you can't win and they know how to pull you in. They feel the need to be right and obtain the agreement of others. They may try to make others agree with them, even if the means is by hurting them with physical force.

Withdrawal: Some children sort of give up. They can't, they won't try, they say I'm sorry a lot, and they often have a reason why they can't do better; they withdraw.

Escape and imagination: I'm an Indian, and Indians don't have to go to school. If life hurts too much, one will merely dream up a new fantasy. There usually is an intense interest in another culture or time zone, another country, a world of animals, and video games. Pretending to be an animal usually involves a dog, a cat, or a hamster.

Social Chameleon: One can mimic another person perfectly, likes to speak in scripts, and enjoys being on the stage when playing a defined role. I once knew a twin who watched Aladdin when he was little and spoke just like Lago the parrot. He sounded like Gilbert Gottfried 24/7 for many years afterwards. He had it down perfect, too. His brother used his own voice.

Chapter 18

WHAT KIND OF THERAPY/THERAPIST SHOULD I GET?

Understand that autism affects cognition, language, motor skills, sensory integration, and social skills. It is likely your child will need a team, so don't settle on only one person to help with all of their issues.

Occupational Therapist
Works on fine motor skills, such as handwriting and sensory integration.

Physical Therapist
Works on gross motor skills, such as walking up stairs.

Speech Therapist
Works on language and pragmatics and teaches the use of language in social situations, such as learning not to be too literal.

It is likely your child will need a team, so don't settle on only one person to help with all of their issues

ABA Therapist

Applied behavioral analysis can help motivate to comply with routines and directions, especially when language skills are limited and/or cooperation is poor.

Counselor or Psychologist

Can help with executive function re-mediation and compensatory strategies, family dynamics, self-esteem, social skills, and emotional recognition and management strategies. Also assists with psychological or neuropsychological testing for an autism diagnosis (can determine or rule out possible additional mental health diagnoses).

Pediatric Neurologist

Can help with a referral for testing if a diagnosis needs to be considered. Assists with basic medication issues and can order an electroencephalogram (EEG) to check for seizures and other types of structural brain imaging, possibly to rule out other neurological issues that may be present.

Psychiatrist

Manages and prescribes medications for more complex cases where mood disorders may be present.

Typically, children start with speech and occupational therapy first. Ideally, one or both of these therapists will integrate therapy within a play group to start teaching social skills early. They work on language use in a real social context and encourage self-regulation in small groups where some small children have a lot of trouble staying calm, still, and engaged. By about age twelve, it is likely that both the speech therapy and occupational therapy will be discontinued.

Your school may provide some of these services. Keep in mind that the school follows an educational model of service delivery. This means that if the child has adequate skills to get in and out of a desk and can make some progress educationally, that's what will be targeted. The medical model, followed by private therapists outside school, is more concerned with getting them to be as good as **they** can be. Private therapists also typically treat longer, more often, and more intensely.

Schools begin serving children with significant difficulties at age three, so if yours is two-and-a-half years old, it's time to call the school for an evaluation to determine what they can do. Often, the higher functioning kids won't qualify, even though they may have been kicked out of several daycares. In kindergarten the teacher had your phone number on speed dial.

Different therapists within the same discipline will have skill sets and personalities that vary. Don't be afraid to experiment with switching around some, as each may have something unique to offer your child that others do not. In terms of personality, look for someone who is firm, confident, adaptable, and patient. If your kid is on the autism spectrum and the therapist can't manage their behavior, or gets mad at them for misbehaving, it may be time to try someone else.

Chapter 19

CARE FOR THE CAREGIVER

Caregiver Stress Inventory

Rate from 1–5 where 1 = not true and 5 = extremely true

1 2 3 4 5   I don't sleep well enough.

1 2 3 4 5   I drink too much.

1 2 3 4 5   I need drugs to get through this.

1 2 3 4 5   I don't exercise enough.

1 2 3 4 5   I don't have time or energy for friendships.

1 2 3 4 5   Date? What's a date? (Including with a spouse if you have one.)

1 2 3 4 5   I worry too much.

1 2 3 4 5   I don't have enough energy.

1 2 3 4 5   I sleep too much.

1 2 3 4 5   I don't know anybody in a situation like mine.

1 2 3 4 5   Nobody could understand what my life is like.

1 2 3 4 5   I feel guilty about not giving enough attention to some family members.

1 2 3 4 5   I don't have time or energy for a hobby.

1 2 3 4 5   I feel guilty when I do something for myself.

1 2 3 4 5   Sometimes I wish I or another family member were not here.

1 2 3 4 5   Frequent headaches or stomach aches my doctor can't help with.

1 2 3 4 5   Sometimes I think I just don't care anymore.

1 2 3 4 5   Nobody can care properly for my child besides me.

1 2 3 4 5   I have never had a vacation away from my special needs family member.

1 2 3 4 5   I feel hopeless sometimes.

1 2 3 4 5   None of the professionals know or understand what is going on.

1 2 3 4 5   I don't have any professional support/treatment.

1 2 3 4 5   I have poor eating habits.

1 2 3 4 5   I don't stay in bed when ill.

1 2 3 4 5   I don't get medical checkups for myself when I should.

1 2 3 4 5   I worry about where I will get enough money for the future.

1 2 3 4 5   I am afraid of my child.

1 2 3 4 5   I am afraid I will hurt my child.

1 2 3 4 5   I used to have a strong faith, but now I'm not so sure.

1 2 3 4 5   Other family or friends disapprove of the way I care for my child.

1 2 3 4 5   I always put others' needs before my own.

Do you notice any warning signs? If so, take action. Taking care of yourself puts you in a better place to care for those you love. Nobody knows what you need better than you.

See also "How can a caregiver care for themselves?" to download a Word document containing the preceding stress inventory and what follows: http://intensivecareforyou.com/resources-for-free/

HOW CAN A CAREGIVER CARE FOR THEMSELVES?

- Ask for help
- Exercise
- Yoga
- Meditationn http://intensivecareforyou.com/resources-for-free/
- Relaxation http://intensivecareforyou.com/resources-for-free/
- Start a hobby
- Time with friends
- Support group: Tx p2p
- Counseling
- Hobby
- Watch out for thinking errors (patterns of thinking that keep you stuck or magnify a problem) http://intensivecareforyou.com/resources-for-free/
- Get a pet
- Set goals for yourself in your own dream book http://intensivecareforyou.com/dream-book-getting-clear-want-making-real-now/
- Problem-solve
- Eat better
- Identify obstacles
- Examine and change your story
- Journal

- Take time to rest
- Let others take care of you
- Let others take care of your child
- Daily me time
- Acceptance
- Faith

Know what is stressful for you and take steps to manage those situations. Take a step back and decide how big the problem really is.

Do you spend more time actually confronted with the problem or more time being distressed as you repeat the problem over and over in your mind?

Do you absolutely know for sure that the problem is real, or is it merely a story you tell yourself? Could it be something in the future that has not happened that you fear and mistakenly think you *know* will happen?

Is the problem something you can change or influence, or is it beyond your control and better off accepted?

Leave your ego out; allow others the freedom to follow their own path and learn their own lessons.

Place a check next to each statement below if you would like help in that area:

☐ **Someone to talk to about my problems.**

☐ **Help in dealing with problems with husband/wife.**

☐ **More time to be with my child.**

☐ **Information about my child's abilities.**

☐ **Childcare help.**

☐ **Help and information about behavior problems.**

❑ Better/more frequent therapy services for my child.

❑ Counseling to help me cope with the situation and my caregiver stress.

❑ More information about how I can help my child.

❑ Help with sibling rivalry/jealousy of siblings.

❑ More information about nutrition.

❑ Special equipment.

❑ Friends who have a child like mine.

❑ More time for myself.

❑ More time to be with my spouse or friends.

❑ Someone who understands what I am going through.

Help changing my mindset that:
    ❑ *I'm stuck,*
    ❑ *Things will never change,*
    ❑ *My child won't get better or live independently,*

❑ Nobody can understand or help me.

What else would you like help with?

❑ _____

❑ _____

❑ _____

❑ _____

LIST OF HELPFUL RESOURCES:

Who Says Men Don't Care?
Gambone, James, PhD, Rhonda Travland, MS, 2011
www.MaleGuideForCaregiving.com

How To Be a Resilient Caregiver
http://lifework.arizona.edu/ec/caregiver_manual_now_available_online

The Caregiver Helpbook: Powerful Tools for Caregivers
Schmall, V, Cleland, M, Sturdevant, M, , Legacy Health Systems. (2000)
www.powerfultoolsforcaregivers.org

Passages in Caregiving
Sheehy, Gail, Harper Collins, 2010

ORGANIZATIONS:

Family Caregiver Alliance
National Center on Caregiving
785 Market Street, Suite 750
San Francisco, CA 94103
(415) 434-3388
(800) 445-8106
Website: www.caregiver.org
E-mail: info@caregiver.org

Autism Speaks https://act.autismspeaks.org/

Autism Society of America http://www.autism-society.org/

Autismlink
https://autismlink.com.au/ http://www.autismlinks.co.uk/

Children and Adults with Attention-Deficit/Hyperactivity Disorder (CHADD) for Attention-deficit/hyperactivity disorder (ADHD) support groups

National Alliance on Mental Illness (NAMI) https://www.nami.org/ for bipolar and mental health support groups

Care.com lists people who can care for special needs children or seniors in your area

Community Resource Coordination Group (CRCG): In Texas, each county provides a community resource coordination group. This group connects people or families with local public and private agencies to help families caring for children with intense behavioral health issues.

Chapter 20

WHAT IF I'M A GRANDPARENT?

First of all, be compassionate and understanding. Yes, you know your son's or daughter's weaknesses and what they should do or should have done to be better. Your son or daughter already knows about your judgments. Keep them to yourself. Understand that sometimes it is very difficult parenting and living with someone on the autism spectrum. Don't tell your offspring how they are failing and how they need to set firmer boundaries, apply more rigid discipline, etc. They need a break sometimes too. This may mean handing their child the iPad or letting them play video games or watch YouTube videos, even when they haven't yet earned the privilege. Be accepting and forgiving while the parent takes a few minutes to relish some well-deserved peace and quiet. They need to pick their battles.

Learn more about autism, and try to spend some time alone with each grandchild. Find out how to enjoy them as they are. See our *Resources For Free* pages for more information that may help you better understand!

Chapter 21

TRANSITION FEARS

What if they are afraid to grow up?

Are you worried they won't be able to live independently, go to college, or acquire and keep a job?

Welcome to the trials and tribulations of being a parent. Watch out for the fear and judgment trap. It might go something like this:

If they don't learn to (fill in the blank) (do as they are told, finish homework, take a shower, etc.), then they will never (fill in the blank) (get a job, find a girlfriend/boyfriend, move out of my house, and so on). And they will (fill in the blank) (end up living in a cardboard box under a bridge).

We are not powerful enough to predict the future. Please remember that the truth is—you don't know what is going to happen.

TIPS FOR PREPARING TO TRANSITION

1. **Goal setting:** Facilitate the identification of long-term goals.

2. **Building confidence:** Put more energy into noticing their accomplishments and what they do right. See the chapter on self-esteem for more tips.

3. **Use their gifts, passions, and special interests.**

Utilize the Dream Book method to help with long-term goal setting and motivation.

This is a beautiful way for a student to establish a sense of purpose and start planting the seeds of what they want to grow in the garden of their mind. (Please also read *Garden of the Mind* by Rebecca Schwarzlose.)

Ideally, a Dream Book will be a special leather-bound book, so it will last—especially when its owner falls asleep with it in bed.

The Dream Book's user should be instructed as follows:

1. On each page, as you think of one, write about a dream you have for yourself.

2. Go to Google Images, or choose other sources of images, such as your own photo library. An even better idea might be to create your own symbol or drawing to represent each of the dreams written in your Dream Book. Tape or paste these into the page with your written description.

3. At night, shortly before you go to sleep, review your dreams. As you arise the next morning, take a few moments to see yourself living the dreams you want.

RATIONALE

1. Writing your goals and focusing on a specific image of the goal helps you to be clear and specific about your vision and intention.

2. Regular dream review helps you stay focused and encourages accountability. This practice also helps to replace negative and discouraging thoughts that can be obstacles.

3. Focus your conscious attention on what you want to create, rather than on your fears and what you are afraid might happen. This helps you harness that 95 percent of mental activity most of us are not aware of. Put this energy to work *for* you. We remember best what we studied directly before we went to sleep the prior night. As we walk through daily life, we can prime ourselves to notice opportunities to realize our dreams and prove that they are already true or are in the process of becoming true. Use the "Dream Book Menu" for more ideas.

MENU OF SAMPLE DREAMS

Get some good images for each page or draw symbols! Try rewriting "I want" as "I am," and rehearse these at least once a day for a week—and then let me know what happens! Instead of the phrase, "I want to be successful," use "I am successful" instead! Use the following categories to help generate more dream ideas.

Aging

I am going to continue exercising and staying fit into my 70s, 80s, and 90s. Rewrite: I am continuing to exercise and will stay fit, long into my 90s.

Work

I'd like to love what I do and make enough to live comfortably. Rewrite: I love what I do and make enough to live comfortably.

Relationships

I want to meet someone who loves me no matter what, knows my shortcomings, and forgives me. I'd like to be with someone I can love back the same way. I want someone who appreciates me. I would like to spend time every week doing something with friends, just for the fun of it.

Love

I am loving/loved without limits.

Mental health

I want to be free from fear and anxiety. Rewrite: I am free from fear and anxiety. I am confident and secure.

Spiritual

I want to connect with a higher power. Rewrite: I am connecting with a higher power.

Physical health

I want to remain free of pain and disease. Rewrite: I am free of pain and disease.

Social relevance

I want to impact the people I live with in positive ways. Rewrite: I am impacting the people I live with in positive ways. I want more and closer friends and colleagues. I am making closer and more friends and colleagues.

Material items

House, geographical location, money, car, Xbox, computer, games, jewelry.

Academic performance
I want to make a reasonable effort and make the grades I need to do what I want. Identify what it is that you want.

Watch out for phrases such as "try my best," or "try your best." If you have someone who thinks like me, and some of the people I see—this creates a terrible dilemma. How do you know when you did your absolute best or what that was actually supposed to look like? You can always look back and say you could have tried harder and worked longer, so how do you know when to let yourself off the hook? My dad always told me that, and I thought about it. If I am running track and I try my best…well, I would be dead at the end, right? If I were still alive, that meant I didn't give it everything I had.

Special interests/achievement: sports; video games; art.

State of mind: to be free from fear and anxiety; to value myself; to feel a sense of purpose.

Obstacles to overcome: doubt; negative thoughts; illness; lack of energy; lack of confidence.

Fantasies?

When your counselee or child perceives you as helping them clarify their dreams and making them come true, you form a therapeutic alliance or an influential and mutually beneficial relationship. Put yourself in the role of the person who helps them make their dreams come true.

After some goals have been written, come back to them and try writing them in the present tense instead of the future tense. There's a trap in the semantics of "I wish…" which might create "I will be happy when…" or "I don't" or "I'm not." For example: I will be happy when I have a lot of money; I don't do my best in school; or I'm not exercising and staying in shape. This is an excerpt from *Your Dream Book* (Brad Mason, 2016) a beautiful workbook and visual experience available at www.intensivecareforyou.com.

Consider that at eighteen years old they may developmentally be more like twelve or fifteen, and may not be ready to transition out of your home until they are, say, twenty-four. The timing should not necessarily be classified as "never." However, the transition may occur later than for typically developing peers. Better late than never? Remember, it's not a race.

There was a young man—let's call him Bryan—whom I met in high school. He scored at the very top on an IQ test. At age sixteen he had difficulty knowing how and when to cross the street in front of the school to go to the recreation center. He didn't seem oriented to using the button for the walk/don't walk sign at the crosswalk under the traffic light. He did not look both ways to make sure the street was clear before crossing. Bryan and I practiced this street etiquette many times before he mastered it.

Bryan also didn't seem to quite know what to do with himself during passing times in the hall or in the cafeteria when he was finished eating. He would pace up and down, back and forth, twisting a lock of his hair around his finger, and muttering to himself. He did understand, when I asked him, that people watching him might assume he was "crazy" or something. We began to work on stress triggers, signs, and management strategies. We created plans for what he could do when he finished eating in the cafeteria; he could go to the library and study or shelve books. We worked on walking with a normal gait in the halls, keeping a string in his pocket to twist with his fingers instead of his hair, and what kind of face to make for other students. We agreed upon appropriate, expected comments for passersby. He practiced with, "Hey," "What's up," and "How's it going."

The last time I checked, he was attending a college where he was paired in a dorm with another young man on the spectrum. He was checked on. Bryan graduated, got a job, and then went back to school for a graduate degree. See? You never know.

I later met another student who happened to attend the same high school. Let's call him Henry. His mom worked at the school. Henry was bright, unusual looking, and the best character imitator you ever met. He was brilliant and perfectly matched the voice and posture of the person he imitated. Henry was quite funny, often dark, and easily angered. He definitely didn't like his "special teacher," and didn't care for most of the other students in his social skills class either. He found them annoying and upsetting. He had no tolerance for even minor teasing from them. He began responding with death threats. Then one of the students deliberately provoked Henry until he blew up and punched them in the nose. The school had him arrested, and he went to jail. Henry could not get over the unfairness of it all. His night in jail—they would not immediately release him on bail—was traumatizing.

Henry became darker and even angrier. He began talking about death and wanting to take over the world and control everyone through fear and intimidation. His mother quit her job and pulled him out of school. It just wasn't working. Being a single mom, this was very difficult for her financially. Things were not looking good for Henry and his future. We decided he should try and get a job, and he did, at a pharmacy stocking shelves. Henry loved it. He was good at it. Everything had its place. He was competent and making a little money on his own. With a renewed energy and outlook, Henry finished high school from home, went to college, and graduated—up from the ashes.

Sometimes it does take dramatic change and intervention. Some kids just gradually figure it out. Sometimes one small thing changes, and then everything changes, like Henry getting his job. A total transformation was unveiled—mad to happy, just like that.

I met "Tim" when he was thirteen. Tim was floundering in a private school with an accelerated academic curriculum. He barely made C's and D's, with his parents constantly on him to do his work and turn it in. Tim seemed unconcerned, disengaged, and unmotivated. He was adrift and had few-to-no real friends. In the beginning of eighth grade, Tim was pulled out of private school and placed in a public school. The hope was that the academic load might be a little easier and he could experience himself as more successful in school.

The summer before he began school, Tim spent most of his time in his room playing Minecraft. He was addicted. As soon as school began, his parents set an automatic grade alert for 80 in the school computer's grade portal. They told him that when a grade alert came, he would have to turn in all of his electronics until the grade was above 80 again. Tim didn't like this. He moaned and complained. The first time he lost his electronics, he was curled up in the fetal position crying on the floor. "NO, why, it's not fair," he said. Later, he got used to it. His parents didn't even have to check their email; Tim knew when his grades had dropped. Arriving home from school, he wordlessly handed over to his stepfather his laptop, iPad, and iPhone. Tim preferred to give the items to his stepdad because he was assured of no lectures, shaming, or blaming. The electronics were placed on Tim's nightstand until his grades improved.

You know what? Tim never went more than one day without his treasured screens. Somehow, every time, he not only found out which assignments were missing, he completed and turned them in on time. He also was able to get the teacher to enter the grades in the computer the same day, so he always got his stuff back the next day.

Then his parents pulled a fast one. During the summer after eighth grade, they told Tim, "Since you made all A's and B's this past year, you'll be taking advanced placement classes in the ninth grade." Tim was not happy. "No, why, it's not fair, I don't want to," Tim said. Tim told his parents he wanted to quit the band. His parents pulled another fast one on him. "Okay," his parents said, "But you will have to pick another extracurricular activity. You are not going to sit in your room all day playing video games." Guess what? Tim didn't like this either. He refused to choose another extracurricular activity. And so he was told he would participate in band again, followed by the marching band soon after. His mother said he was curled up in the fetal position, crying on the floor of the SUV on the way to the first day of marching band.

But then he got used to it. Tim still had the same deal about his grades and electronics. He still felt he needed to keep his Minecraft. He kept going to band. He kept his grades up.

Then Tim met a girl in band. He had a girlfriend, and she adored him. Tim started practicing more with his instrument and getting better and better. He became used to advanced placement classes and the kids who attended them. He even hosted a big video game competition at his home, where approximately thirty peers attended. Tim obtained his driver's license and, surprisingly, paid enough attention not to have a wreck. For his sophomore year, he made his schedule himself and turned it in. He showed it to his parents, and he put himself in all advanced placement classes.

Tim began to see himself differently. He decided he wanted to be a doctor. Now Tim is attending a prestigious university on a scholarship. He is in the university band, and so he has a structured social setting to keep him connected with his peers. Do you want to know the kicker? On his own, Tim applied to college, applied for scholarships, and filled out financial aid forms. He had no prompts or assistance from his parents whatsoever. This is from a kid, who at thirteen, had (for years) showed zero initiative and was about as passive and checked-out as you could possibly imagine.

You can't predict the future based on current information. You don't know what it will take, or when it will happen. Most people, when motivated, overcome all kinds of obstacles and "get better."

Maybe it has to do with providing the right supports, the right rules and structure, a random chance love relationship, a teacher who takes an interest, or a change in setting, such as homeschooling or getting a job. You won't know what it's going to be until after it happens and, even then, you really can't be sure why they got it together and became happier, can you?

— Chapter 22 —

VIDEO GAME ADDICTION

Do you have a child who seems lost in his video games? Do they sneak them when they are not supposed to, find loopholes in filtering programs, and fight with you over turning them off? Are they spending tons of time immersed in a digital reality, while avoiding homework and socialization? These are your signs!

The problem is that the video games begin to be valued over parental approval and relationships. Socialization and homework are seen as interruptions and avoided. Your child may be daydreaming about video games in school, as well as acting them out on the playground, instead of receiving instruction. How will they learn the skills and rewards of the real world if they aren't participating?

ARE ALL OF THEIR FRIENDS DOING IT?

Your child may argue that all of their friends are doing it and that they can't talk to their friends if they don't join the online games. You may feel uneasy about the time they spend playing games, thinking about games, and watching games on YouTube. You may be unsure about where to set boundaries and what is reasonable.

IS BEDTIME A TANTRUM?

Your child may be bullying you into buying them games and letting them play them, even past their bedtime, with the threat of a terrible tantrum. This is baloney. This is harmful to you and your child. Letting them have everything they want does not fit with your idea of parenting.

TRUST YOUR INSTINCTS

Be smart and learn to trust your instincts when it comes to parenting. Reach out for help if you are unsure of anything. You can engage a counselor, family members, or friends to help you define some structure around reasonable limits. You may wish to discuss how to deal with the fits and arguments, as well as talk about creating rewards and consequences that will help your kid reset to habits that will lead to improvement in their mental and behavioral health.

- How can you monitor and manage your children's use of the internet?
- Do you think it's a good idea to let them have the internet connection in their room or should they be in a family common area where their use can be supervised and monitored?
- If you have ever accidentally Googled links to inappropriate sites, what are the odds your child might also?
- How do you know if your kid has a video game addiction? Do they sneak playing and break rules in order to play? Do they get in trouble over playing? Does playing video games interfere with their schoolwork? Does it interfere with their relationships with peers or family members, like you? That

sounds like an addiction to me. Does an alcoholic keep booze in their house? Why or why not? Codependence and enabling means you buy into the idea that they NEED their video games to be okay. How is this possible?

I can see the idea that they can become dependent and think they need them. Is this healthy? Human beings have lived and thrived on this planet for a very long time before video games came along. These games are unique to this generation. I believe that this means we can be okay without them. My children know that if they don't respect the rules about internet use and video games, or if they end up causing us too many problems, I am okay with getting rid of them. I certainly don't need my kids to have these things.

If you have a child on the spectrum who is young, I would advise you to be quite wary of letting them play too much. I often hear parents, of children who are older, lament that there is nothing else their child enjoys doing—no other reinforcer—and it is the only way they can unwind and escape. How did this happen? I'm pretty sure we had kids with autism spectrum disorders before video games were invented, and those children found a way to make it. If you are only just beginning the war with your child over electronic use, watch out!

I recently worked with some very nice parents who were struggling with fights over video games and electronics use. They reported having these difficulties for several years, trying different ways to manage the behavior, and approaching different counselors. Their teen-aged son tried every way possible to get his phone from his parents, or borrow their phones, so he could play his favorite video game. When they tried to get him to turn it off for dinner or bedtime, arguments, refusal, cursing, and even physical altercations resulted. I told them if they wanted to fix the problem right now, we could do that.

I told them not to loan their phones to him anymore. Then I said, "Give me his phone." They handed it over, and I put it in my drawer and asked if they were ready to call 911 if their son became dangerously unmanageable. They said they were ready. Their son was not pleased. We decided to try thirty days—thirty good days—without significant behavior problems—which would be tracked daily on a calendar we printed. After the thirty good days, he could have it back with limits we established, and any violations would result in losing the phone again for a longer period of time.

After the first two weeks, I saw them again. Their son had achieved eleven days towards trying to manage his phone and video game use. He had been more polite, more pleasant, and much more willing to perform chores, do homework, and comply with family routines, including bedtime. School had gone well also. He had been more social and active in the community.

Some children are just not able to handle this electronic, digital stimulation. The gaming and digital consumption seems to change their personalities on the days they partake. Usually once they become adults, they are better able to set limits for themselves. I also have known many families who fought this type of losing battle throughout childhood and adolescence. Do you want to continue fighting for years, or end the war now?

Chapter 23

MASS SHOOTINGS

Consoling Your Child or Teen
Through Times of Terror

The mass shooting in Las Vegas on October 1, 2017 was unbelievable. In today's world it is nearly impossible to shut off a child's fear-engendering exposure to media coverage of such tragic events. A person on the autism spectrum is prone to perseveration (getting stuck on something bothering them), excessive fears, obsessive-compulsive tendencies, and difficulty regulating emotions. As such, news of such events can be quite traumatizing.

I met with a teen just yesterday who confided that they were now afraid to go to movie theaters, concerts, or really any public gatherings for fear that someone might open fire on them. How do you help someone overcome such a fear?

1. You can help them choose a mantra or affirmation for fear as a way to counter thoughts and feelings of terror. http://intensivecareforyou.com/resources-for-free/ has a list of "Affirmations to Calm Fear" to give some examples and ideas.

2. Encourage self-care through the adoption of healthy habits, such as exercising in the morning, which restores and maintains feelings of well-being in the brain chemistry that promotes happiness.

3. Be open to discussing the problem with them and allowing them to feel and think the way they do. Don't just tell them they shouldn't feel that way.

4. Let them know that you are taking care of them, and the chances of them becoming a target in a public place is very, very low.

5. Limit media exposure.

6. Review how our elected officials, the CIA, FBI, the military, the police and their helpers are working together to make our world safer and prevent these things from happening again.

7. Maintain normal routines.

8. Review safety procedures at home and school, such as helping them identify at least one person in each setting that they trust and can go to for support.

9. Keep an eye on their emotional state and take them for professional counseling if their normal life continues to be disrupted by their fears.

10. Take care of yourself and model bravery by not giving in to fears yourself.

Chapter 24

MY CONCLUDING COMMENTS

Remember that love and happiness are acts of faith, courage, and discipline.

Faith is when you choose to believe in something, even if direct evidence has not yet supported your belief. This is a belief you have committed to and don't look back on. You believe the child you care about is going to be okay, they will learn and change, and they will adjust and adapt. You can't know the timing to their successes, but you will be right there, patient and smiling, when they happen. Take this action to heart and make your leap of faith if you haven't already; your child will be able to interpret your emotions from your posture, words, and tone of voice. Do not give in to fear, for whichever path you choose:

1. Fear, criticism, and judgment; or
2. Faith, love, and support,
   you will be leading them alongside you.

Courage means that you keep going, even when you are afraid; you remain steadfast in your thinking and behavior in the pursuit of your goals and values.

Take this action to heart and make your leap of faith if you haven't already

Discipline is taking personal responsibility for your thoughts, feelings, behavior, life, and the changes you want to make. These alterations begin with your thoughts and feelings and are accelerated by your practice of mastering your state of being. There is no waiting or blaming, for this is the life you have. This is the one and only moment you live in, right now. Work hard and be willing to do that which may at first feel uncomfortable for you in the pursuit of a prioritized life.

The reason I have detailed the difficulties someone on the spectrum is expected to have is to promote understanding, effective interventions, and most especially to address a concern of mine. I do not like it when a person is judged and labeled as making "bad choices" or having a defective character when they, in fact, lack the confidence and thinking skills they need to adapt successfully to the demands of the environment. This type of judgment is demoralizing, devaluing, and doesn't help anyone do better.

I want you to become that person for someone else who always has compassion, always thinks well of them, and continues to encourage and support them, even when unexpected behaviors are occurring. Hopefully, you had at least one person in your life who you knew always saw you as your highest self. You realize how powerful you can be by allowing yourself to be completely loving. If you can remember someone you knew in your past who influenced you with the gift of unconditional positive regard, you can see and feel how their loving influence has stayed with you for years after the gift was initially given. These masters of positive influence shared the most valuable thing they had to offer—themselves. Likewise, realize that the most valuable thing you have to offer is not the ability to understand a variety of complex intervention strategies and resources, the most value you can add to a person who struggles is yourself, your positivity, love, supportive regard, and encouragement.

Discipline yourself to not give in to fear, criticism, or judgment when you interact with this person. Project your positive regard into the words you choose to speak, your tone of voice, your body posture, and your facial expressions, and you will give them a gift that keeps on giving. Sew and you shall reap. Be careful and intentional about what kind of seeds you are planting. Know you are imparting a lasting gift that stays inside the person, comforts them in times of stress, dismay, and doubt, and elevates the way they think about themselves.

APPENDIX

WHY AUTISM?

One of the questions I am most often asked is, "Why is the prevalence of autism so much on the rise? How could we go from 4 in 10,000 to 1 in 100?" I believe the rise in autism in our country sends us some very clear and important messages—about ourselves. First, we are being led down the path of exploring what it means to be human in a social context, that is, how we are supposed to behave and think in relationship to other people. It is a journey with the potential for us to define and reshape who we are and how we want to be. It is an opportunity to challenge cultural trends that encourage egocentrism (thinking only about ourselves), trends that encourage anxiety, and the drive to always want more.

In other cultures, as well as in ancient history, children with neurological disorders became shamans. They were allowed to live away from the group and be different. They were cared for in terms of food in daily living, and their unique thinking styles and abilities contributed to the welfare of the group. When the tribe encountered a problem they could not solve, they brought it to their shaman for answers. There was no effort to make different people the same as everybody else, as we do now in western culture and educational institutions. We try to make different people in to the image our culture says people should be, adhering to rigid and abstract standards, ignoring reality. I call this the autism of the system.

We can learn to be people who think about others, and we can learn how to accept ourselves as we are rather than always feeling as though we must have more. We must increase our possessions and wealth, and we must always be getting something to improve our status, or we are not worthy. WE could learn to be more flexible and accepting.

From an evolutionary perspective, perhaps nature or God throws out individuals that are extremely different from time to time. Maybe sometimes it works out and sometimes it doesn't. But take a look at how different Edison was. As a child, he had extreme difficulty socializing during school. Now, think about the contributions he gave to the world. Where do you think rocket ships, computers, and electric light came from?

Finally, these children may be serving as another type of early warning system. Their heightened sensitivities to toxic byproducts of modern industrialization and current mass agricultural practices and the degradation of our food may be predictive of what we all have in store for us if we don't read the signs and change our habits. We must take care of our planet and take care of ourselves. This is the message they bring, a warning and a signpost to better mental and physical health practices, a better society and culture. It is a message we are sending to ourselves.

SIGNS OF ASPERGERS SYNDROME

Aspergers syndrome (AS) has been removed as a clinical category of "mental disorder" from the Diagnostic and Statistical Manual of Mental Disorders (DSM-5), which means it is no longer a clinical diagnostic category with a corresponding code that can be used to receive reimbursement for therapy and treatment in the United States. However, since approximately one million people in the United States consider themselves "Aspies," and this is a population that resists change, the term is unlikely to drop from our common vernacular anytime soon. AS is characterized by difficulties in social interaction and narrow or restricted patterns of interest. This may include failure to use eye contact, develop peer relationships, and share enjoyment with others as expected. You may also see preoccupation with parts of objects, intense focus on a particular subject such as dinosaurs, Pokémon, a video game, weather, or Thomas the Train, inflexibility in routines, and repeated motor mannerisms. Some people have some of the characteristics, but not all, and may be diagnosed as PDD-NOS, ADHD, OCD, or bipolar.

Social anxiety and difficulty recognizing, communicating, and managing emotional responses are also frequently seen in this population. Many of these people are socially interested and have good intentions and are at times very sensitive, yet lack the cognitive flexibility and social communication and thinking skills necessary to navigate the social world gracefully.

They often seem unaware of unwritten social rules until explicitly taught; they don't "get it" as naturally as their neurotypical peers do. Often we see high intelligence and vocabulary, a collector of information on a specific topic of interest, and terrific long-term rote memory coupled with difficulty with everyday problem-solving skills. They may neglect to develop social curiosity about what other people are thinking, failing to realize that other people have a different mind with different interpretations, intentions, and feelings. They may seem only aware of one mind—their own.

Language may be atypical, with unusual pitch, volume, prosody, and/or rhythm. You may hear monotone, sing-song, or the little professor ("Well, actually…"). Then a monologue ensues that may continue long after the listener has shown signs of disinterest or even left the room! Use of language may be literal and concrete, coupled with the failure to interpret jokes, idioms, and figures of speech. Attempts at entering into groups may be characterized by off-topic remarks or quotes from a favorite video.

Motor skills may be delayed. Difficulty riding a bike, tying shoes, and writing are commonly seen.

RESOURCES

Attwood, T. 2007. *The Complete Guide to Asperger Syndrome*. London: Jessica Kingsley Publishers. [This is a complete guide by one of the foremost experts in the world on this topic.]

Dawson, P. and Guare, R. 2009. *Smart but Scattered*. New York: Guilford Press. [My favorite resource about executive functions, with checklists to help pinpoint which brain skills are weak and how to remediate or compensate. If smart but scattered describes you or someone you love, get yourself this resource.]

Grandin, T. 2006. *Thinking in Pictures*. New York: Vintage Books. [Brilliant book and great read. I'm not sure everyone who has autism thinks just like the author, but definitely worth reading.]

Myles, B., and Southwick, J. 2005. *Asperger Syndrome and Difficult Moments*. Shawnee Mission, Kansas: Autism Asperger Publishing Co. http://www.asperger.net. [Great resource if you are suffering from meltdowns.]

Riggs, Nathaniel R., Jahromi, Laudan B., Razza, Rachel P., Dilworth-Bart, Janean E., and Mueller, Ulrich. 2006. *Journal of Applied Developmental Psychology*. July–August; 27(4), pp. 300–309.

Schonfeld, A.M., Paley B., Frankel F., and O'Connor M.J., Child Neuropsychology. 2006. December; 12(6), pp. 439–52.

SOCIAL SKILLS AND SOCIAL THINKING CURRICULUM

Gutstein, S. 2002. *Relationship Development Intervention with Young Children*. London: Jessica Kingsley Publishers. [Great active fun games for younger children to learn to enjoy play!]

Howlin, P., Baron-Cohen, S., and Hadwin, J. 2002. *Teaching Children with Autism to Mind-Read*. West Sussex, England: John Wiley & Sons Ltd. [Curriculum to help children understand desire-based emotion, situation-based emotions, false belief, and perspectives of others.]

Madrigal, S., and Winner, M. 2008. *Superflex… A Superhero Social Thinking Curriculum.* San Jose, CA: Think Social Publishing, Inc. [This would be my top recommended curriculum for teaching flexible social thinking skills.]

Walker, H., McConnel, S., Holmes, D., Todis, B., Walker, J., and N. Golden. 1983. *The Walker Social Skills Program.* Austin, TX: Pro-Ed. [One of the few programs out there with empirical support; involves video, role-play, and behavioral coaching/management of skills taught outside of the social skills teaching place.]

Winner, M. 2002. *Thinking About You Thinking About Me.* San Jose, CA: Michelle Garcia-Winner, SLP. http://www.socialthinking.com. [Heavy reading, but it will help you understand how these kids think.]

Winner, M. 2005. *Worksheets! For Teaching Social Thinking and Related Skills*. San Jose, CA: Michelle Garcia Winner, SLP [Great, especially if you have lots of skills to teach all school year long.]

Winner, M. 2005. *Think Social*. San Jose, CA: Michelle Garcia Winner, SLP. [Great, especially if you have lots of skills to teach all school year long.]

Winner, M. 2008. *A Politically Incorrect Look at Evidence-based practices and Teaching Social Skills.* San Jose, CA: Think Social Publishing, Inc. [If you want to get into the arguments about whether it is appropriate to use educational resources to teach social skills and explore whether teaching social skills can work, this is for you.]

Winner, M. 2008. *You Are A Social Detective.* San Jose, CA: Think Social Publishing, Inc. [A must for younger children who don't understand about keeping their bodies and minds in the group.]

BOOKS FOR EXPLAINING AUTISM OR ASPERGERS TO A CHILD

Faherty, C. (2000). Asperger's…*What Does It Mean To Me? A workbook explaining self-awareness and life lessons to the child or youth with High Functioning Autism or Aspergers.* Arlington, TX: Future Horizons, Inc.

Gerland, G. (2000). *Finding Out About Asperger Syndrome, High-Functioning Autism and PDD.* Philadelphia, PA: Jessica Kingsley Publishers, Ltd.

Gray, C. (1996). *Pictures of Me.* Jenison, MI: Jenison Public Schools. (www.thegraycenter.org)

Hall, K. (2001). *Asperger Syndrome, the Universe and Everything.* Philadelphia, PA: Jessica Kinsley Publishers Ltd.

Jackson, L. (2003). *Freaks, Geeks & Asperger Syndrome: A User Guide to Adolescence.* Philadelphia, PA: Jessica Kingsley Publishers Ltd.

Lawson, W. (2003). *Build Your Own Life: A Self-Help Guide For Individuals With Asperger's Syndrome.* Philadelphia, PA: Jessica Kingsley Publishers Ltd.

Newport, J. (2001). *Your Life Is Not a Label.* Arlington, TX: Future Horizons, Inc.

Vermeulen, P. (2000). *I Am Special: Introducing Children and Young People to their Autistic Spectrum Disorder.* Philadelphia, PA: Jessica Kingsley Publishers Ltd.

Vicker, B. (2003). *Disability information for someone who has an Autism Spectrum Disorder.* Bloomington, IN: Indiana Resource Center for Autism.

Willey, L.H. (1999). *Pretending to be Normal: Living with Asperger's Syndrome.* Philadelphia, PA: Jessica Kingsley Publishers, Ltd.

BOOKS FOR EXPLAINING TO CLASSMATES AND SIBLINGS

Welton, J. (2003). *Can I tell you about Asperger Syndrome?* Philadelphia, PA: Jessica Kingsley Publishers Ltd.

Etlinger, R. (2005). *To Be Me: Understanding what it's like to have Asperger's Syndrome.* Torrance, CA: Creative Therapy Store.

Meyer, D. (1997). *Views from our Shoes: Growing Up with a Brother or Sister with Special Needs.* Bethesda, MD: Woodbine House.

Elder, J. (2005). *Different Like Me.* Philadelphia, PA: Jessica Kingsley Publishers Ltd.

Wong, A. (2009). *In My Mind: The World through the Eyes of Autism.* Mustang, OK: Tate Publishing.

Ellis, M. (2005). *Tacos Anyone?* Austin, TX: Speech Kids Press.

Keating-Velasco, J. (2007). *A Is for Autism, F Is for Friend.* Shawnee, KS: Autism Asperger Publishing Company.

Coe, J. (2009). *The Friendship Puzzle: Helping kids learn about accepting and including kids with autism.* Bluebell, PA: Larstan Publishing.

SOCIAL GROUP PARTICIPATION AND HEALTH LINKS

Jetten, J., Haslam, C., Haslam, S., and Nyla Branscombe. 2009. Scientific American Mind. Sept/Oct 2009 20(5). Scientific American, Inc. pp. 26–33. [Turns out withdrawal is not good for your health, and being in groups is.]

Putnam, R. 2000. *Bowling Alone: The Collapse and Revival of American Community.* New York, NY: Simon & Schuster.

COGNITIVE-BEHAVIORAL STRATEGIES FOR HIGHER FUNCTIONING PEOPLE WITH SOCIAL LEARNING DISABILITIES AND SELF-REGULATION PROBLEMS

Attwood, T. 2004. *Exploring Feelings.* Arlington, TX: Future Horizons, Inc. [Great workbooks that teach skills for managing anger and anxiety.]

Attwood, T. 2008. *The CAT-Kit.* Arlington, TX: Future Horizons. [Therapist tool for teaching emotional regulation skills.]

Avery, R. 2008. *Meet Thotso, Your Thought Maker.* Smart Thot, LLC. [Teaches younger children the idea of making Band-Aid thoughts for your boo-boo thoughts to help yourself feel better.]

Buron, K.D., & Curtis, M. 2003. *The Incredible 5-Point Scale.* Shawnee Mission, KS: Autism Asperger Publishing. [Terrific technique for mapping out the gradations in an emotional response and developing emotional awareness and coping.]

Buron, K.D. *A "5" Could Make Me Lose Control!* Autism Asperger Publishing Company, Shawnee Mission, KS. http://www.asperger.net.

Gray, C. 1994. *Comic Strip Conversations*. Future Horizons Publishers: Arlington, TX. http://www.futurehorizons.com. [Effective way to visually teach appropriate language and prediction of perspective and emotion.]

GAMES FOR SKILL-BUILDING

Escape From Anger Island (ages six to twelve). Instant Help Publications. [Strategies for anger.]

Fib or Not (ages ten and up). Gather Around Games, Inc. [Using and interpreting affect, understanding deception; an important real-world skill.]

Gameskidsplay.net. [Tons of outdoor games to help build speed of processing and cooperation.]

Hullabalu (ages four and up). Cranium, Inc. [Great for young kids learning to follow directions.]

Imaginiff (ages ten and up). Crystal Lines [Great for teaching thinking about others' skills.]

Kid Cranium SpongeBob (ages seven and up). Hasbro [All of these Cranium games help develop communication, especially nonverbal communication skills.]

Land of Psymon (ages eight and up). Western Psychological Services. [This game teaches categories of thinking errors, such as extremism. It also teaches how to recognize unwanted and inaccurate thoughts and replace them with smarter, healthier ways to think.]

Moods (teen/adult). Hasbro. [Builds affective and emotional intelligence/vocabulary.]

My First Therapy Game (ages six to twelve). http://www.childtherapytoys.com. [Good for stimulating conversation and as an ice-breaker.]

The Talking, Feeling, and Doing Game (ages four to fifteen). Creative Therapeutics. [May help broaden and deepen concepts around what feelings are and how they can be predicted by context.]

Too Much, Too Little, Just Right (ages five to twelve). Creative Therapy Store [Helps to teach skills to discriminate the appropriate size of a reaction, amount of volume, and degree of animation.]

Ungame. http://www.talicor.com. [For ages up to eighteen; facilitates getting to know one another.]

Any charade game is good too!

ORGANIZATIONS

Autism Speaks (US)	https://www.autismspeaks.org/
Autism Speaks Canada	http://www.autismspeaks.ca/
Autism Science Foundation	http://autismsciencefoundation.org/
Autistic Self Advocacy Network	http://autisticadvocacy.org/
Autism Research Institute	https://www.autism.com/
Autism Cares Foundation	http://autismcaresfoundation.org/
Global Autism Project	http://globalautismproject.org/
National Autism Association	http://nationalautismassociation.org
Temple Grandin's Resources	http://templegrandin.com/
Asperger/Autism Network	http://www.aane.org/
Spectrum News	https://spectrumnews.org/
Autism Citizen	https://autismcitizen.org/

Autism Now	http://autismnow.org/
Autism Canada	http://autismnow.org/
Geneva Centre for Autism (Canada)	https://autism.net
National Autism Center	http://nationalautismcenter.org
Canucks Autism Network (Canada)	https://canucksautism.ca/
Organization for Autism Research	https://researchautism.org
American Autism Society	https://myautism.org/
National Autism Network	http://nationalautismnetwork.com
A.J. Drexel Autism Institute	http://drexel.edu/autisminstitute/
NEXT for Autism	https://nextforautism.org
Autisable	https://autisable.com/
Ted Lindsay Foundation	https://tedlindsay.org/
US Autism and Asperger Association	http://usautism.org/

RISE Scholarship Foundation	http://risescholarshipfoundation.org
Autism Spectrum Disorder Foundation	http://myasdf.org/site/
Jaden's Voice	http://jadensvoice.org/
Lawyer's Autism Awareness Fund	https://thelaaf.org/
International Society for Autism Research	http://autism-insar.org/
Doug Flutie Jr. Foundation for Autism	http://flutiefoundation.org/
Potential Inc.	https://potentialinc.org/
Autism Service Dogs of America	http://autismservicedogsofamerica.com
Grant a Gift Autism Foundation	http://grantagiftfoundation.org/
Global and Regional Asperger Syndrome Partnership	https://grasp.org/
Generation Rescue	http://www.generationrescue.org/
Daniel Jordan Fiddle Foundation	https://djfiddlefoundation.org/
First Signs	http://www.firstsigns.org/

Holly Rod Foundation	http://www.hollyrod.org
The Autism Research Foundation	http://theautismresearch-foundation.org
Simons Foundation: Autism Research Initiative	https://www.sfari.org/
Project Autism	http://projectautism.org/
National Autism Network	http://nationalautismnet-work.com
Sesame Street Workshops	http://sesameworkshop.org/what-we-do/our-initiatives/autism/

ABOUT THE AUTHOR

Bradley Keith Mason M.Ed., LSSP, LPC, LPA
Licensed Specialist in School Psychology
Licensed Professional Counselor
Licensed Psychological Associate

Brad Mason has worked in public schools for twelve years as a Special Education Counselor and Licensed Specialist in School Psychology. Prior to that, he worked in a brain injury hospital with both adults and children as a Behavior Therapist.

Mr. Mason has been in private practice as a Licensed Professional Counselor for fifteen years and operates the Autism Clinic and Family Counseling Center in downtown Georgetown, Texas. He currently works with children, adolescents, adults, and families in groups and individually. He specializes in treating children with social skills deficits and emotional regulation problems. Mr. Mason is the author of the Intensive Care for You video course series, available as videos on Amazon Prime and as video courses at Intensivecareforyou.com, created to help leaders of children who struggle to guide and discipline in more loving and effective ways.

Mr. Mason has completed a Bachelor's Degree in Psychology and English, a Master's Degree in Education for School Psychology, post-graduate education at St. Edward's University, as well as ongoing education in treating Autism Spectrum Disorders, Family Dynamics, Career Counseling, and Advanced Counseling Techniques. Mr. Mason has conducted and published research, in conjunction with various authors, in the fields of aggression, gender role stereotypes, and children's television. Mr. Mason has presented his work for the Southwest Conference on Human Development, and offers presentations and staff development to school districts and various agencies. Frequently provided workshop topics include:

- **Counseling Tools for Kids in Schools**

- **Behavior Management at its Best**

- **Counseling Strategies for Kids with Autism and ADHD**

- **Anxiety and Children**

- **Anger and Children**

- **Teaching Social Skills Through Play.**

These topics and more can be viewed in greater detail at http://www.bradmasoncounselor.com/workshops/

Mr. Mason has also authored *Your Dream Book*, *Counseling Tools for Kids in Schools*, and *My Power Book*.

COUNSELING TOOLS FOR KIDS IN SCHOOLS

By Brad Mason

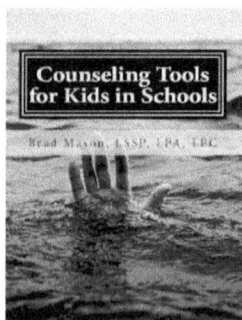

You don't have time to do research, find materials, and make a plan for your counseling sessions. Kids need more structure and support for counseling. You're busy answering calls, making schedules, filling out forms, attending meetings, doing evaluations, and making reports. You care about the kids and you want to do something engaging, productive, and useful in your time with them. They can be hard to reach and teach—these children with autism spectrum disorder, ADHD, or serious emotional disturbance. The difficulties these children have with emotional and behavioral control can be devastating to their futures and highly disruptive in their families, friendships, and classrooms. You need ready-to-go forms, templates, and strategies. Lists of resources, handouts for teachers and parents, reviews of games and books that can help you help them would be great too. Whether you are in private practice, employed in a school, or just beginning to look for more tricks and new tools, you can now get what you need. Start creating successful, observable behavioral and emotional outcomes.

FIVE STARS

By Jenna Fleming on January 30, 2016

> *"Brad shares a wide range of resources for school-aged children in a format that can be used with individual students, groups and as resources for parents and teachers. I am a school counselor and can use it as a go-to resource for most cases in schools. There are quite a few behavioral therapy ideas in here that can easily be applied in schools. All very doable and rooted in good solid theory. Included also are ideas for writing goals with lots of specific examples, a pretty large section on emotional management, which comes up quite a bit in schools. There's some really good information in here on executive skills, sensory issues and social skills, which is great since resources for school counselors are pretty sparse."*

YOUR DREAM BOOK
By Brad Mason

YOUR DREAM BOOK
Brad Mason LPC, LSSP

Your Dream Book is going to become your journal of goals and inspiration that will take the place of your doubts, fears, and self-imposed limits. Dreams have no limits. Your limits are created by your conscious mind. Therefore your fears are not genuinely real; they are only as real as you make them and carelessly believe them into being.

You will begin to feel as though you are living your dream NOW. Instead of saying to yourself, I will be really happy when, or could be doing really well if, you will be thinking I AM.

How can you know you are realizing your dream—your goal—if you don't first know what it is, it's description, appearance, and what it feels like? Create and practice this internally and watch it happen outside of you "in reality." Use Your Dream Book to get clear on what you want and make it real.

MY POWER BOOK
By Brad Mason

MY POWER BOOK
Brad Mason

This is a book written for adults to learn more about how to increase their personal power in ethical and humanitarian ways. *My Power Book* is about using your power for good. It is not about gaining power over others to manipulate them into giving you what you want against their wishes. It will help you recognize and escape the clutches of someone who uses coercive unethical means to have power over you. Recognize and overcome ways you give your power away. This is also a book for learning stories and strategies for handing down this invaluable wisdom to children. How do you balance parental power with empowering your children to thinking for themselves? Create a legacy you can be proud of. Start your revolution today.

www.ingramcontent.com/pod-product-compliance
Lightning Source LLC
Chambersburg PA
CBHW020005290326
41935CB00007B/306